Concepts of Karate

The Karate of Toru Takamizawa & Steve Rowe

The Budo Classics N. 4
Concepts of Karate -The Karate of Toru Takamizawa & Steve Rowe
by Steve Rowe

Copyright © 2023 The Ran Network

First Edition

Publisher: The Ran Network
info@therannetwork.com
https://therannetwork.com

Front cover photo: © Caroline Reynolds

Cover and layout design: Simone Chierchini

ISBN: 9798866738540

Imprint: Independently published on Amazon KDP

Steve Rowe

Concepts of Karate

The Karate of Toru Takamizawa & Steve Rowe

The Ran Network

TABLE OF CONTENTS

I dedicate this book to Toru Takamizawa, my karate teacher, because of the 'giri' (obligation) I still feel toward his memory 25 years after his passing: his teachings are at the root of everything I teach today. He was a genius and great character who became 'a person in heaven' far too soon.

I would also like to dedicate it to my wife Ann, daughter Caroline, granddaughter Rhianna and son-in-law Mike, who are also an integral support network for me, my martial art studies and business. How they put up with me, I'll never know.

My thanks to Mike and Cerys Ames for being my photographic models for parts of this book as well.

Finally, to my students, too many to mention and many of whom have been with me up to fifty years.

FOREWORD

It is with great honour and some trepidation that I have been asked to write the foreword for this book. While my writing style is often described as "business-like" at best, I cannot help but feel a deep connection to the subject matter and the author himself.

Nearly half a century ago, I joined Steve's club as a scrawny, inexperienced beginner. I had recently been brutally beaten in a pub car park, and my confidence was shattered. The training at Steve's club was rigorous and demanding, pushing me to my limits both physically and mentally. I vividly remember the barefoot runs through the streets of Greenwich and later around the dog walkers' track in Dartford. The intense workouts, including exercises that would now be deemed too dangerous, tested our endurance and resilience. And then there was the sparring, where I learned the true meaning of martial arts respect from Jackie, a formidable black belt who showed me that strength and skill have no gender.

Throughout the years, I have followed Steve on his journey, training with various instructors and immersing myself in the world of martial arts. Steve's commitment to continuous learning and growth has been an inspiration to me and countless others. He has encouraged me to train with different instructors, broadening my horizons and deepening my understanding of the art.

The evolution of martial arts has been profound, with a newfound focus on the integration of mind, body, and spirit. Steve's research and exploration of the internal aspects of martial arts, rooted in Buddhist principles and meditation, shed light on the deeper dimensions of the practice.

The principles and teachings shared in this book are not limited to martial arts alone; they hold value for anyone seeking personal development and growth. Steve's coaching technique is methodical, well-researched, and easily assimilated. His teaching strategies, meticulously recorded in this book, have the potential to guide and inspire countless practitioners.

Toru, a deeply influential figure in both Steve's and my journey, left an indelible mark on our understanding of martial arts. His coaching techniques, introduced over three decades ago, still resonate with us today. Toru possessed a rare combination of linguistic, martial arts, and scientific knowledge, enabling him to explain the "why" and "how" behind techniques. His innovative approach, coupled with the traditional "old school" methods of challenging students, set him apart as a true master.

I recall a particular instance during one of Toru's courses when he brought a whiteboard and asked the students how Hooke's Law applied to kicks. His gaze fell upon me, and I became the unwitting recipient of his question. From that moment on, whenever the whiteboard appeared, I knew I would be put to the test.

My first trip to the Czech Republic with Steve remains etched in my memory. On the first morning, he surprised me by announcing that I would be teaching the session, leaving me to sink or swim. It was a testament to his belief in my abilities and a reflection of his own teaching prowess.

Both Steve and Toru epitomize the fusion of modern coaching strategies with traditional martial arts. They were and continue to be ahead of their time, their contributions deserving of recognition and preservation.

I wholeheartedly recommend this book to anyone practicing martial arts. Its contents are not only useful and enlightening but also a testament to the dedication and passion that Steve and Toru have poured into their craft. May this book guide and inspire you on your own journey of personal growth and mastery.

Martin Gatter is an 8th Dan Karate and Tai Chi International Coach having trained under Steve Rowe for 50 years.

PREFACE

In this captivating book, Steve showcases his intellectual prowess by taking the ideas of another martial arts disciple and transforming them into brilliant gems. He recognises the importance of creating an organisation that can withstand the test of time, even when its founder is no longer present. The text at hand is a testament to the profound teachings of Toru Takamizawa, showcasing the structure and depth of his wisdom.

Although this book revolves around martial arts, its relevance extends far beyond the fighting arena. Steve delves into the profound aspects of life and the various endeavours we pursue, often encountering failure along the way. Through his eloquent and captivating narration, he takes readers on a remarkable journey spanning from the mid-forties of the 20th century to the present day. This voyage is a rare source of wisdom, exploring the dark corners of human character within 'bullying' style fighting clubs, while also celebrating the quality martial arts *dojo* found across the UK and the world. The journey begins in Nagano, Japan, and continues to unfold in Chatham, UK, highlighting Toru's analytical skills and Steve's profound expansion of his mentor's ideas.

This book is not a mere translation or regurgitation of Toru's teachings; instead, Steve proves himself to be a worthy sparring partner, elevating the concepts to a new level of depth and structure. His dedication to sharing Toru's wisdom is evident in each chapter, which begins with a carefully crafted seed of teachings from Toru. Steve then nurtures these seeds with his own observations, research, and the outcomes of his and Toru's passionate teachings throughout the years and various locations. Every chapter culminates in a unique clause of wisdom, applicable to both the dojo and everyday life.

Beyond its martial arts focus, the book also imparts life's most precious lesson – how to be a great student. It provides readers with precise instructions on how to continually improve oneself, surpassing yesterday's version. In a time filled with empty promises and distractions, Steve's guidance on thriving in today's hectic world is invaluable.

The idea for this book emerged during a serene moment in Cobtree Manor Park, where Steve and I sat on a sunny mid-June Saturday, engrossed in conversation for hours. The vibrant nature surrounding us invited contemplation and served as inspiration. As one of the fortunate few who had the opportunity to read the manuscript before its release, I can attest to the profound impact it had on me. I encourage you, dear reader, to immerse yourself in its words, meditate on its teachings, and let it become a part of your everyday training and life. Allow it to transport you and join us in this enlightening conversation.

Robert Musil is a barrister and partner in a leading international consultancy firm, is not only accomplished in his professional life but also in the world of martial arts. As a medallist in the WKC European and World Championships, he has proven his skill and dedication. Additionally, Robert has served as the national karate coach for the WKC and IKU Czech team, mentoring several World and European Champions.

CHAPTER ONE

Background

In karate we talk a lot about styles and lineage, yet we have very few ways of honouring it. I think it's important to honour your roots by explaining where and from whom you learned and documenting it where possible as it keeps our ancestry alive: not in a dry, dusty, historical way, but with stories, tales and legends that keep students interested. When I look at *karateka* I used to be able to tell their lineage by their techniques, principles and etiquette. As time has passed it's now difficult to do that, as lineage is nowhere near as clear as it used to be. Stories and legends are often exaggerated, and that's okay if we appreciate that and are able to extract the teachings from them. After all, we have fairy tales, sutras and parables that we know are untrue but teach us and our children valuable lessons.

This book has gone through a few incarnations before reaching you. At first I wanted to honour Toru Takamizawa by putting together his teachings from the books we wrote together and published under the TAKRO (Takamizawa and Rowe) name. The books were very much of their time and consisted of a lot of charts and translations, and when the interesting parts were put together and modernised, there wasn't enough for a book. I didn't want to 'pad it out' so I nearly stopped there. However, I started to think about 'giri' (obligation) and how no one else has fully acknowledged and attributed Toru's influence, despite him having significantly developed the knowledge of Japanese culture, karate and its terminology, and the politics and coaching methods of so many in the UK.

It made me realise how much I really owe to Toru and how much he has influenced not just what I teach today but also how I teach it. So I put the two together and took around a hundred photographs and ended up with what looked like a book and a Japanese dictionary of karate terms as an appendix. It still didn't

look right, so I scrapped that.

What we've ended up with takes us right back to the original idea for the books we did entitled 'Concepts Of Karate'. I've stuck to the concepts that Toru devised and the methods he taught and how they changed my way of thinking and training, how they have developed in me and my studies.

I think that you will enjoy the way it flows with depth of knowledge, the great stories including all the changes we made, and the information that you will find difficult to get elsewhere.

CHAPTER TWO

How Wado Ryu Came to the UK

First, let's look at the background to the style that Toru taught and how it arrived at our shores along with the reception and cultural mix. Wado (the way of peace and harmony) Ryu (school) has its roots in Shindo Yoshin Ryu (sacred willow spirit/heart school) ju jutsu (the technique of softness) going back in Japan to Akiyama Shirobi Yoshitoki in 1530. The 'willow' came from a meditation he had watching the way a willow tree yielded to the power of nature to let the snow slide off its branches when it became too heavy.

Wado Ryu was founded by Hironori Ohtsuka who had trained in ju justsu from the age of four and Shindo Yoshin Ryu from age thirteen. This style employed the skills of swordsmanship, so the intelligent use of body evasion (*tai sabaki*) and vital point striking (*atemi waza*) was heavily utilised, along with the usual locks and throws that one would expect from ju justsu. This led to Ohtsuka's interest in the striking aspects of karate and of Okinawan masters Funakoshi Gichin, Kenwa Mabuni and Choki Motobu. When first registering his style with the Butokukai, Ohtsuka gave the name Akiyama Yoshitoki as the founder.

It is this background that gives Wado Ryu the unique Japanese *budo* influences and skills that the other styles don't have.

When the Japanese karate instructors first came over to the UK, there was a definite culture clash. It's hard for people these days to understand how the Japanese viewed us and how we viewed them back then.

It was only around twenty years since World War Two. In 1969 I was in the London Fire Brigade and in my crew most had served in the war. My father and his friends had also served. Some had

Previous page: the Shikon dojo shrine with photos of Hirinori Ohtsuka on the left and Toru on the right

been in Japanese prisoner of war camps and most of us knew others who had suffered in the same way.

Not many Japanese had migrated to the UK, and living close to Brixton, in South London, I knew many black people but had never met a Japanese person. Most people I knew still hated them with a vengeance, and when karate was first introduced it was called 'dirty Jap fighting' by many, because our national sport was boxing and kicking, gouging and hair pulling was not seen as acceptable.

I remember a Dutch iaido instructor who stayed with us during an Iaido summer camp in the eighties. He was in his seventies, had been a prisoner in a Japanese prisoner of war camp and been tortured mercilessly, he had to catch rats to eat to stay alive. The camp commander was a kendo practitioner and made the entire camp practice every day. After the war he amazingly kept it up for the rest of his life and was on the seminar with all the top Japanese instructors. An amazing man.

During the mid sixties, karate was introduced into our household when my brother started training in Wado Ryu with Tatsuo Suzuki. I found Japanese *kanji* (Japanese writing using Chinese characters) exotic and intriguing and the Japanese instructors mystical in this strange art. With the advent of the Bruce Lee movies in the seventies, the art exploded with dojos crammed full everywhere.

Japanese culture was very different to ours and therefore acclimatisation was gradual. Okimitsu Fuji, my iaido instructor, told me that in Japan if an instructor liked you he would beat you to make you improve; if you weren't beaten in a session you thought you'd done something to offend him. When he came to the UK he did the same to his students and couldn't understand when the good ones that he'd been beating left! In Japan you didn't ask questions, you followed instructions blindly and trusted the instructor had your interests at heart. A famous Japanese saying is 'if a nail sticks up, knock it down'. Japanese would always talk about themselves in the third person, Toru never wrote 'I' but always referred to himself as 'the author'. I think the defeat of Japan in the Second World War had injured their national pride deeply and they clung to the samurai culture and its ferocity, ironically making them powerful karateka. The other irony is that their success in the west was due very much to Bruce Lee whose films inevitably showed the Japanese as the villains because they considered the Chinese as the 'sick men of Asia'.

The Japanese were also very class conscious amongst themselves and when a group visited the UK they would bring someone over who would take all their business cards and work out in what order they could be introduced. They found western people as mystifying as we did them. I remember Toru standing in front of a mirror teaching himself to smile; despite being a linguist I remember his confusion when a student apologised for his absence because he'd been 'burning a candle at both ends', and another that was late and apologised saying he'd been 'running around like a blue arsed fly'. Toru started collecting these sayings for other Japanese people to help them understand westerners. I read of another Japanese instructor teaching students to 'punch like a wolf': this was passed on for years before they realised he actually said 'punch like in golf', referring to the body twist!

Takamizawa Toru Kyoshi always insisted on being called 'Toru', in the western fashion. This showed why he was so different from the other Japanese *sensei*: in many ways he seemed to fit easily into western society but in other ways he retained his Japanese roots. He once told me that he felt like Gulliver in Gulliver's Travels and that he didn't really fit in anywhere, stranded between two worlds. In Japan they considered him too western (because he had an English wife) and in England he was considered too Japanese.

He was born into a family of samurai lineage in 1942 in Nagano, Japan, one of seven children, and began practising judo at school earning his black belt. At university he studied English and Russian languages and started training in karate under Jiro Ohtsuka, son of the founder of the Wado Ryu style of karate, Hironori Ohtsuka. He told me that his family were disgusted at him training in the art as they saw it as a 'blue collar activity' and one practiced by thugs and the yakuza. He was a very talented karateka, working hard and gaining black belt in just nineteen months and second Dan just eighteen months later.

In 1966 he moved to England and joined Tatsuo Suzuki and his team of Japanese instructors. In 1970 he settled at the Temple Karate Club as resident instructor in Digbeth, Birmingham (which is where I started taking private lessons with him). The Temple club became one of the leading teams on the karate tournament circuit, spawning many of the top competitors and future instructors such as 'The Cat' Birmingham's World Champion Eugene Codrington, Chojinkai Founder Doug James, Coventry's Graham Tuckey and Barry Tatlow and Middlesborough's Cliff Richmond to name a few. In 1975 he met Tracy and became a British citizen. In 1978 he broke away from the other Japanese instructors and formed the first 'multi style' karate association 'Tera (Japanese for Temple) Karate Kai'.

CHAPTER THREE

How We Met

I started training in the very early 70's in a South London karate club under the tutelage of ex army boxer turned karateka, Jim Fewins. At that time the club was part of the Za Zen Karate Kai association, with the Zen Shin Ryu style of karate formed by Jon Alexander, an enigmatic character of shrouded linage that had opened clubs all over the South East of England. Jim was a tipper lorry driver for Penfolds in Lewisham and quite fiery tempered; this led to quite a bit of violence in and round the club. I had a few concussions and many black eyes, broken and cracked ribs, damaged knees, shoulders, finger and toe joints. When I had surgery because of breathing problems, I was told that my nose had been broken five times, I had also suffered a cracked cheekbone and several broken teeth. With my background and the fact that I was working in the security trade at the time, I didn't really think it was that unusual.

Jim didn't pull his punches in any sense of the word and one of the most valuable lessons I learned from him was that 'everyone bleeds', there was no reason to fear anyone, and he certainly lived to that motto. During a visit by Chief Instructor Jon Alexander, Jon bullied one of our brown belt teaching assistants and Jim threw Jon out of the club. We broke away from Za Zen and formed the Greenwich Karate Kai. My black belt exam consisted of being locked in a room with Jim and the other black belt at the time, Dick Clark, who both laid into me mercilessly, no mitts, or padding and it was non-stop– if I stopped fighting for any reason I'd fail. It was 'street' from start to finish, from fighting my way out of corners, off the floor and not stopping for injuries. Looking back, it was crazy and many times, after injuries, I wanted to give up but couldn't, because I knew there was something deep down inside of me that wouldn't let me fail. That black belt was the hardest earned physically, mentally and emotionally, and probably my proudest moment.

In the security world I'd risen through the ranks to become an Operations Manager of a substantial company and had to spend a lot of time meeting clients. I couldn't keep turning up with black eyes and various other injuries and by this time I also had a family and so it was time for a change. I eventually left Jim and formed my own clubs in North Kent. After a while Jim approached me to take over his clubs as he had become a long distance lorry driver driving all over the world.

Suddenly I had several clubs across Kent and South London and was a breakaway from a breakaway with no real official lineage. When Toru formed the Tera Karate Kai, it was the first multi style karate association that anyone could join. It was a brave move on his behalf, firstly to break away from his own Japanese sensei and then because up to that point all the karate groups in the UK were single style and politically very controlling. Perfect timing for me though, to move from a 'street' style of a mixture of karate and kickboxing toward the more traditional Japanese style of Wado Ryu Karate.

Jim had graded me to nidan (second dan black belt) and I thought I'd better regrade under Toru to give the grade some legitimacy. I failed and asked why, to be told that I 'was using a sledgehammer to crush a grape' and that was probably a good analogy, as at the time I did a lot of body building and gym work along with a brutal style of karate. I approached Toru and asked him what I had to do to improve and he told me that I would need private lessons with him.

That started years of driving from Chatham in Kent up to the Temple Karate Centre in Birmingham for private lessons, and most weekends I'd make the trip again for seminars and tournaments. Toru told me that when I started taking private lessons he hated teaching me because I was clumsy and awkward and tried everything he could to make me stop: he made me stand on one leg kicking for ages and endlessly repeat basic techniques. The problem was that I was used to pain and thought I was being taught traditionally, like in the movies! Over time we gradually developed a friendship.

A young Steve front right, with his first instructors

CHAPTER FOUR

How We Formed the
Takamizawa Institute of Karate

Toru's relationship with money was really bad: it embarrassed him and he gave responsibility to others without any oversight. One day, when I arrived for my private lesson, he was really depressed. It turned out that although he was the head of a huge organisation, he was broke, in debt, owed the taxman a fortune and was about to lose his house. He didn't spend recklessly, the money was obviously going elsewhere. I didn't ask too many questions but got him a good solicitor and accountant. It emerged that TERA was a limited company controlled by others, so I had to get him out and away from those controlling him and the money, and put him in charge of his own finances and business.

We arranged for him to get a mortgage on a new build in Chatham by offering him a job in our business and giving over his house in Kidderminster. We arranged for him to teach our black belt classes and opened new clubs for him to teach. We formed the 'Takamizawa Institute Of Karate' with me as Chairman and had all monies sent directly to his house, so he had complete financial control. I was able to get TIOK accepted by the Governing Body (the English Karate Council) as I was the Secretary and subsequently the Chairman of it at the time.

Everything was set. All Toru had to do was to resign out of TERA and we decided that he would make the announcement at the TERA AGM held at the Summer Course in Rhyl in Wales. When the time came, Toru stood and said "erm… erm… Steve's got something to tell you" – and walked out the room! I had to make the impromptu announcement and tell everybody that Toru was resigning as Chief Instructor of TERA, was forming the Takamizawa Institute Of Karate, moving from Kidderminster to Chatham and that if anyone wanted to stay with him they would have to pay him directly. As you can imagine, that went down like a lead balloon; most went reluctantly over to TIOK and I and my students were forever like the 'red headed stepchild' in the association that we had helped Toru form.

To promote Toru and his unique teachings we arranged for seminars every month on different subjects like tournament fighting, different kata, various Wado Ryu pairs work and refereeing. Toru started each one with "before you can fight, do kata, pairs work, referee (whatever the seminar was titled), you must understand good basics, junzuki hidari gamae (left junzuki stance), kette junzuki (kick and move forward to the next junzuki), 'ich! (One!)'"... Most of the seminar would then consist of the same basics and his 'codes for movement', I was frustrated

at the time, but trying to get my own students to grasp the fundamental ideas of movement before learning the more advanced, I now sympathise with his approach and understand him better. You can't run before you can walk.

It's not what a student wants, it's what they need: a genuine coach will insist on this for the good of the student. A big problem with business oriented martial arts instruction these days is where students are often entertained more than they are taught.

To document his ideas and raise money for him, we decided to write books and self publish under the TAKRO (Takamizawa and Rowe) name titling the series 'Concepts Of Karate', the first being on 'Tsuki and Keri' and the second on 'Uke and Tachiwaza'. This was in 1986, when we only had one of the first Amstrad computers that had to be loaded up with DOS (the operating system) using one floppy disk and then worked on another containing software and files. There was no internet, no digital cameras and no printers. We had to type it on the Amstrad, photograph on film, get the photos drawn and put everything on gestetner stencil before having it hand printed on a gestetner machine in a friends's garage, then staple the book together to sell on seminars, in clubs and by post. Books quality was certainly 'of their day' but the contents were gold dust! A lot of that information is contained in this book as a part of my 'giri' (obligation) to Toru as my teacher.

We often travelled together to teach and for other events. Toru was a terrible driver, he took the driving test seven times before he passed and drove everywhere, even on motorways, at fifty miles per hour. When travelling abroad he would insist on wearing a suit and tie to 'look professional' and the irony was that he was always stopped and searched at customs whereas in my track suit I would always walk straight through!

He had OCD that contributed to his genius in karate technique and was a hygiene freak to the extent that when we stayed together, even if I and my wife had cleaned, he'd always do it again. He was never a fan of our pets, telling us that dogs and cats should live outside and that our rescued sparrow would be eaten in Japan. He was horrified when he first met our German Shepherd dog.

He liked a drink and we had many a late night on vodka martini's with lemonade and Toru singing in over thirty languages. When it came to the Japanese National Anthem (which it inevitably did) I usually went to bed! Despite any differences we always got on well together; he often stayed at our house and was good company.

To prevent further animosity from the group toward myself and my students from when we formed TIOK, Toru and myself decided that I would leave and form Shi Kon, but we remained friends until his death, sometimes travelling together for separate

seminars in Norway.

In 1998, aged 57yrs, Toru passed away from throat cancer, survived by his wife and their four children. He left a gaping hole in the world of karate and in the hearts of many students, but also a great legacy that thrives to this day. I have many great stories of our time training, travelling and teaching together and I will thread some through this book and remember them all forever.

CHAPTER FIVE

The Genius of Toru Takamizawa

Toru didn't see 'styles' of karate, he just saw movement. His genius was that he would study the movement and codify the essential parts so that if a student learned and followed the codes, they couldn't do the movement wrong. He saw the human brain like a computer: if you press a key on a computer, a screen full of information would come up, by using codes like 'K1, K2, K3 and K4' with each code, all the information you need would be attached in your mind. This meant that in both learning and teaching, no essential qualities of a technique were missed. When grading students it was a simple task to notate the codes that were required for them to attain the standard or what they needed to work on to improve.

He understood the importance of co-ordinating the body with the two hemispheres of the brain; the fact that the right brain instructed the left side of the body, and that the left brain instructed the right side of the body; that both sides couldn't function at the same time but the speed of interchange created co-ordinated skills; that the ability to connect and time the upper body with the lower also gave timing, speed and power. He knew how to use the body to build up potential energy and when and how to release it as kinetic. Considering this was the 80's, he was way ahead of his time.

While others were beginning to call karate kihon (basic technique) and line work 'archaic', Toru understood that they were a doorway to develop left and right and upper and lower co-ordination, that using science, physics and anatomy taught to a moving body how to apply plyometrics to utilise the potential and kinetic energies. That kihon was the best way to learn, apply, test and critique these skills. The way he codified the movements and skills meant that students were able coach themselves even when they were on their own. This also changed 'training' into 'studying'.

Toru was in my estimation the fastest, most fluid and effective karateka out of all the Japanese sensei around in the UK at the time. All of the others had great technique and spirit and we were particularly blessed with the choice that we had in the UK, but because of Toru's ability to analyse movement and power, it put him in a league of his own. For a man of small stature, he

not only moved blindingly fast and easily but also carried an immense amount of power.

He was very careful with his use of language. He realised that words like 'strength' and 'aggression' led to negative tension and an unnecessary stiffness in movement, so would rather use 'force', 'energy' or 'spirit'. He taught us to be careful with the terms 'relax' and 'relaxation' because of their connotation with laziness and he replaced them with 'no excessive tension'.

All of my teaching now revolves around the use of 'keywords'. Each keyword is a label on the door of a room in the student's 'memory palace', so as they get more information relating to those keywords and gain a deeper understanding, they can keep adding to that room for the rest of their life. This is why I can pull a plethora of information from my mind without notes or plans, as all I need to do is take a stroll around my memory palace and everything I've ever learned is still there safely locked away and filed under other keywords in those rooms.

A good example of this is the 'Eight Principles' listed on my dojo wall:

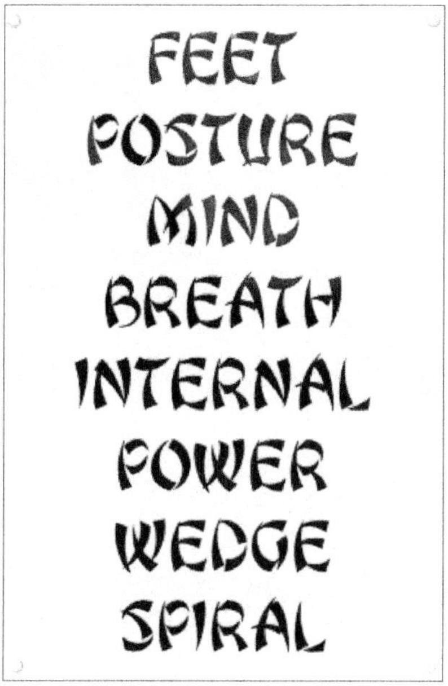

FEET
POSTURE
MIND
BREATH
INTERNAL
POWER
WEDGE
SPIRAL

If all eight are in place, whatever technique you do, it will work and you will remain powerful; if you break one, the rest will fail and the technique won't work. These are the roots of my entire system and the way I categorise, remember and teach it all originate from Toru. You will see this as we go through his karate system.

Feet

We start with feet because they dictate our root, mobility and balance, they are the source of both internal and external power.

They dictate distance from the opponent, the angle of alignment of both our power and direction. The arches of the feet are the first pumps of our internal energy (*ki* in Japanese, *chi* in Chinese). This will be explored in Toru's teaching in the section on 'tachi-kata'.

Posture

If your postural alignment has structural integrity, you will have what the Chinese call *peng* (ward off energy) and the Japanese *kamae* (structure with attitude). You will have a natural, connected, effortless strength. It's one thing to have this in static mode and another to be able to maintain it in movement. This is why a training syllabus must be well layered.

Breath

Learning how to breathe well seems to cause a lot of misunderstanding in the martial arts. It's important to learn how to breathe naturally and apply it. Okimitsu Fuji told me that when you throw a ball for a dog, it brings it back panting and you assume he's tired, but an hour later you're still throwing the ball and the dog's still bringing it back. This is because the dog still has a third of it's breath in 'reserve' and is only topping it up with the panting. So it is for us: if in combat we lose that reserve breath, we start to chest breathe, 'heaving' the chest up and down. We disconnect upper and lower body, our eyes go dead, we change from 'fight to flight' emotionally and our skin colour drains.

A more experienced fighter will often let the younger and more inexperienced fighter burn his energy out by attacking recklessly and he will then look for those signs. He knows that as soon as his opponent's lost control of his breathing, he is weak, drained and disconnected, so he can now attack and win. Toru would advise us to watch for movement in the opponent's chest.

To learn your natural breathing rhythm, it's important to learn where the centre point of your balance is located. This is called the *seika tanden* and it's normally found three finger widths below your navel and in the centre of the tanden (lower *dantian* in Chinese). We move from that point to move in a co-ordinated way–Toru would say 'body moves legs', relating to a baby's first steps. We also breathe from this point drawing the diaphragm down to allow the lungs to fully expand. Many people say 'breathe from the stomach' but you also need to utilise the sides and lower back. Don't breathe in until your body breathes in for you, and don't breathe out until your body does it for you. If you watch anyone breathing whilst they are asleep you'll notice that they breathe in this manner. Breathing is the one function that connects the sympathetic and parasympathetic nervous systems: we can control our breathing with our mind, and when we don't think about it the body takes over. This is the one way we can effect some control over our internal health.

This breathing method calms the body, emotions and mind, connects upper and lower body and means that you can remain aware, focused, and control and understand your breath.

Mind

The mind has four qualities: aware, focused, sensitive and intense. Toru would jokingly say that it's 'the hardest muscle in the body to train'. Take away any of these qualities in the opponent and everything else collapses: if you are able to distract them, allow them to get lazy, or dissonant, they are lost. Maintain these in yourself and you remain in control, intensity is the guardian of all the others.

Power

You can see how interrelated all these keywords are. If your feet are in the right place, the right angle and distance and working properly, if the body is aligned in the most connected powerful way, if you are able move applying plyometrics and putting your body weight into a technique and releasing all your other potential energies at the right time, you will have maximum power.

Internal

Your internal power relies on being able to access the deepest parts of your body, manipulating the spine from the feet and legs, through the core, and opening the energetic lines through the body, with no excessive tension. This of course depends on all the other principles to make it work.

Wedge

The wedge gives us the 'when and how' to meet the opponent's force and wedge through it like the prow of a ship through water, deflecting their technique, displacing their lines of power and striking them in one movement. We will explore this further in Toru's teachings on *uke*.

Spiral

Spirals are continuous motion, never leaving a 'dead spot' in motion and always generating power. At the wedge point, it also gives us the option to meet the opponent on a curve, so that we can stick, follow and redirect - think of how difficult it is trying to hit a spinning ball.

Each one of these principles is based on Toru's 'hook' technique derived from how a computer works, and is a label on the door of a room in our memory palace that we can spend a lifetime investigating. You will see them cropping up again and again in this book.

CHAPTER SIX

Self Defence and Karate

To understand the relationship between self defence, street fighting and the art of karate I think we have to take a broad enough perspective. My transition from 'kickboxing street fighter' to classical Japanese budo practitioner had a few moving parts, the main one in karate was of course Toru, then there was Okimitsu Fuji in iaido; I took many years of weekly private lessons with both teachers, and at the same time I was studying Buddhism with Amaravati and Chithurst monasteries that provide a lot of quality material. Shinto Buddhism is the root of philosophy in traditional Japanese martial arts and in my opinion it's impossible to learn them well without understanding the culture and philosophy that permeates them: it's in the name of the arts and styles of all the traditional martial arts. The name 'Karate' originally meant 'Chinese Hand'. Funakoshi changed the kanji for *kara* to mean 'empty' (as in *karaoke,* meaning 'empty orchestra') with the 'empty' having the Zen connotation of 'empty of intention'. *Te* was a generic term for martial arts but directly translated as 'hand'. Thus 'karate' came to mean 'empty hand' and in the Zen sense of 'empty of any intention' martial art. The *do* added on to the end is the same as the Chinese '*tao*', meaning 'the way' (that the entire universe arises and returns to). 'Karate-do' is therefore the martial art that is the way of peace and harmony.

This gives a better understanding of the much vaunted phrase *'karate ni sente nashi'* (there is no first attack in karate). It is for self defence both philosophically and also tactically advantageous. In the tai chi classics, the three cardinal sins are to 'protrude, collapse and lean', as any of these would destabilise the practitioner's structural integrity and give the advantage to the opponent. This is why in some of the old kung fu movies you'd see the two opponents take a kamae facing each other and days go by as they waited for the other to move and create an opening. This awareness is called *zanshin* and translates as 'remaining mind'.'

Teaching bodyguards, police and security personnel, I have to make the point that these days everyone carries a camera and CCTV is everywhere, so we have to be very careful, aware of the law and always assume that we are being filmed. The way we may have responded years go is probably invalid these days. It's important to not raise hands first, it's important to always be aware; our peripheral vision plays a vital role because it means that we are able to perceive all around us and our natural threat awareness is activated. Like when we drive our car, we scan the road ahead and are able to risk assess and react accordingly, we can use the same mind in threatening circumstances. This is known as *enzan no metsuke*, to 'look at the mountains behind and see everything in the foreground'. It means you are unlikely to be tricked or fall for a feint. This 'scanning the horizon' can be seen at the beginning of *Naihanchi kata*.

Our soft skills play an important role by giving a potential

attacker a way out of the situation they've got themselves into. A good security/police officer will often be able to defuse most situations before they get violent. Particularly if the attacker can sense that behind that calm polite front is a strong, well trained, resolute back.

As I said earlier, it's important to not raise hands in any way that can be

Naihanchi kata

46

perceived as a threat. Any trained person can raise hands in time to a real threat; by taking a natural 'blade' half facing stance there is little target for a potential attacker. Using the 'karate ni sente nashi' strategy you can allow the attacker to 'protrude' with a strike, thereby creating an opening so that you can raise an open hand to their face wedging and deflecting the attack. You are only asking them to 'stop' and they may 'run onto your defensive hand'. The 'wedge' can then be turned into the 'ball'

continuing the deflection and the attack can be neutralised with a lock, throw, strangle or choke using the energy they initiated. Every situation is different and an aware, focused, sensitive and intense mindset is required to spontaneously react in the best way coupled with the right kind of skill set.

Karate is first and foremost an art. It's also a sport. Post World War Two, the Japanese founders had to prove to the American occupying forces, like Kano had done with judo earlier on, that karate was not a revolutionary threat, that way they could bypass the national ban on martial arts. Like judo, Karate was developed as a sport and copied the same format of uniforms grades and sporting rules, coupled with kicks from savate and punches from boxing to make it more visual. The original form of karate was essentially a grappling art of self defence and its deadly roots were still hidden deep inside for anyone who had the mind to explore.

From a self-defence point of view, using the Zen philosophy, introduced by Funakoshi and combining its grappling techniques, karate is actually a perfect mix for today's self-defence making the practitioner not a 'fighter' but a capable 'peacemaker' who won't end up in prison.

For years karateka would go to the dojo and follow the ritual of putting on their white 'pure' *karategi* (karate suit) and tie their *obi* (belt) around their waist, tying the knot tight against their seika tanden (energy centre); bow to the *kamiza* (dojo shrine) and then to the sensei (the one who has ready trodden the path to learn the 'way' and can therefore guide you) as they enter the dojo, to clear their mind to be ready to learn. When line bowing to the kamiza, kneeling down (*seiza*) and bowing to the sensei again, the sensei would call for a period of meditation with the command "*mokuso!*"

My problem with this was that no-one in karate ever taught me what we were supposed to be doing during this period. We'd all be keeling there, often in pain, just waiting for the command "*mokuso yame*" (stop meditating). When I asked anyone what we were supposed to be doing or how to meditate, no one could give me a satisfactory answer. I found exactly the same in the Zen art of iaido. Also in tai chi we would be practicing *zhan zhuang* (standing like a tree) and receive a lot of physical instruction but absolutely nothing about the mind and emotions.

I knew that this must be the most an important part of our training because it was imbued into every ritual and name within these systems. It wasn't just the westernisation of the arts because even my Japanese and Chinese instructors couldn't teach me or anyone else I knew in these arts! How could this be so? I still couldn't control my mind and emotions, I didn't have that internal locus of power, external factors like other people and situations could too easily disrupt my *wa* (peace). How could I resolve this?

This led me to looking outside of the martial arts to find the answer. I recalled the Shaolin Temple in the TV series 'Kung Fu' and the bits where the screen would go wobbly as it went into the past and Master Po would dispense the wisdom I was looking for to Kwai Chang Cain. Thus, I turned to it's underlying culture of Buddhism.

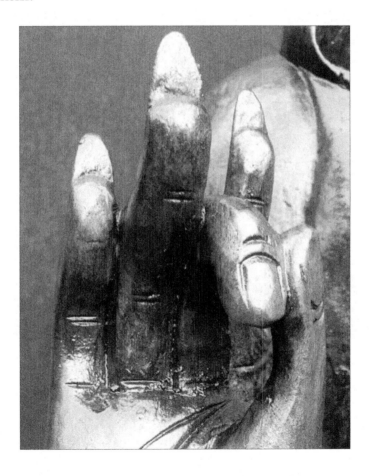

CHAPTER SEVEN

Buddhism

In this light, let's take a brief look at the philosophy and culture that underlies karate and other Japanese budo. Incidentally, the kanji for budo is to 'stop the spear', making the peacemaker title even more relevant. The name of every art and style carries reference to this, 'wado' the way of peace and harmony, 'iaido' the way of mental presence and immediate reaction, 'kendo' the way of the sword, 'aikido' the way of harmony with universal energy. It permeates the arts from top to bottom.

Buddhism also uses keywords and phrases that contain an enormous amount of depth. The Buddha was a genius in the sense that when he became fully enlightened, he realised the problem that he would have trying to teach what appeared radical in the day. Many of his students wouldn't be able to read or write and some would be princes and kings, so he picked the one subject that he knew they would all be able to relate to – suffering. He chose four simple 'noble' (because they would ennoble a person) truths:

1. There is suffering
2. There is a cause of suffering
3. There is an end of suffering
4. The eight fold path

Each truth has to be studied and understood.

The eightfold path is is split into three parts, wisdom, ethics and concentration. The first two relate wisdom, the next three ethics, and the last three meditation.

1. Right perspective
2. Right resolve
3. Right speech
4. Right behaviour

5. Right livelihood
6. Right effort
7. Right mindfulness
8. Right concentration

Each part of the path has to be lived and balanced. As karateka we need to have a broad perspective. The saying 'the mind of a bigot is like the iris of an eye, the more light you shine on it, the more it contracts' means that we have to constantly expand our mental horizons, embracing empathy, compassion, patience, tolerance and kindness, otherwise we contract. Resolve is a keyword for us as karateka because it's too easy to give up without it. Each training session is a penny in the training bank, good or bad, it's all a part of our path forwards and a learning experience–day after day, week after week, month after month, year after year eventually makes us rich in understanding, insight and wisdom.

Our behaviour, our speech, the way we earn a living are important to us. We shouldn't cause harm with any of them and it's important to contribute to our family, community and environment.

The last three are to do with meditation: too much or too little effort and we fail, understanding the middle path is essential; to maintain a state of mindfulness and concentration allows insight to arise, the power of learning and trusting our instincts and insight leads to a harmonious path with ourselves, our community and environment.

I feel this is a perfect code of conduct for all karateka.

The three characteristics of existence are:

1. All things are impermanent
2. All things are unsatisfactory
3. All things are not self

These are keywords to be studied and understood. The one thing that never changes is that everything is always changing. The Buddha likened it to trying to grasp fire: it's good to look at and enjoy, but the moment you try to hold on to it you'll get burned.

You cannot be permanently satisfied by trying to hold on to or even avoid anything, you will suffer if you want to have or not have anything. Letting go is like holding a stone: you could hold it palm down and then drop it and many people think this is what's meant in Buddhism by 'letting go,' or you could hold it palm up and still let it go. Life with the proper type of engagement is a joy.

What we think of as a 'self' is just a part of the machinery and software of the body. The 'software' (thinking mind) evaluates but doesn't store, and the 'hard disk' (subconscious) stores but doesn't evaluate; however, it's just machinery. We are not that self, but the consciousness that is observing through the machine. Alan Watts, the renowned Zen 'beat' philosopher, insightfully described us as 'an aperture through which the universe observes itself'.

The three jewels in the crown that assist enlightenment are:

1. Buddha (the one who knows)
2. Dharma (the truth of existence)
3. Sangha (a group of like minded people)

A perfect code for the life of any martial artist. Buddha is not actually a person but the state of being awake and fully engaged in the conscious stream of life. 'Woke' is currently being used as a derogatory term but, used correctly, it's a state of being fully conscious, engaged and insightfully aware of the truth.

Dharma is the truth. People often talk about 'your truth' or 'my truth' but they really mean 'your or my opinion'. Truth is eternal and unchanging, that which nourishes our universe and what we need to be awake to.

Sangha is a like minded group of people on the same or similar path that help to nourish your being. This is the function of your 'dojo' (place of learning 'the way') and association.

The 'mon' for Shi Kon (our logo) is a dharma wheel with eight

spokes to represent the eight fold path and four circles to represent the four noble truths.

I'll never understand why meditation, emotional intelligence and character development are given lip service in all the martial arts and in every advert for them and yet no-one is actually teaching how to do it. The problem then is that it's reflected in every discussion, where it inevitably falls into 'but would it work in the street' and testosterone fuelled arguments about uncontrolled violence. Which leads to instructors behaving like school bullies and students that have gone to clubs because they've been bullied getting bullied again. We see far too many instructors delivering unnecessary pain to a compliant student and then strutting around like they've just performed a miracle.

Mindset is something often discussed in karate and I've heard terms like 'emergency mindset', 'pre-emptive' 'flinch response', 'aggression' used and never felt comfortable with these negative terms. This is why it's good to look at the philosophy, culture and nature of the arts: 'peacekeeper' is a positive term, 'emergency mindset' is that of a victim, while 'hunter's mindset' is that of the predator and can be utilised to bring a situation to a peaceful resolution by 'hunting' it. If training is done in a negative, aggressive manner, it must deplete skill. If we look at how animals when young learn to hunt and defend themselves, they play, rolling and wrestling in a positive, playful way. Put two young children together in the garden and within minutes they'll be rolling around together. Old tribal and village interaction always contain wrestling, chanting and dance interactions.

As humans we need to bring our inner animal out to play, just like training a puppy or child. Our dojo needs to be a 'puppy class', where we learn to socialise and play enthusiastically with others. This is why push hands and grappling works well with humans, it's our natural method of interaction and if the instructor encourages a positive mindset of courtesy and enthusiasm with a 'hunter's mindset' for a desired outcome, ending with an act of courtesy like a bow, handshake or fist bump, it works much better. Remember that Funakoshi said that 'karate begins and ends with courtesy'. Like 'there's no first attack in karate', there's far more depth than first meets the eye.

In tai chi I was taught by Jim Uglow, also a Hung Gar kung fu teacher, who has a great understanding of the kung fu and tai chi culture and he kindly took me to Hong Kong for private lessons with Ma Lee Yang, the Yang Family lineage holder.

These days I mainly teach tai chi but the structure of my teaching and underlying principles of movement and power rely on keywords, memory palaces and principles of movement and brain function, which is why the way I teach tai chi is unique in those circles. There are many common ideas and principles from the tai chi classics that unify Toru's teachings with the way I teach. Having learned from him first meant that I already had insight into many of the classics.

CHAPTER EIGHT

The Structure Of Kata

Many years ago I wrote a poem about kata, to embody my thoughts. Ironically, when I posted it on social media many people read the first line and made negative comments not realising that if they'd have read the whole poem it was saying the same as them…

Is Kata A Waste Of Time?
Is there a point to doing kata?
Or is it just a waste of time?
Does it have an application?
That is magical and sublime?
By the time it came from China,
To Okinawa and Japan,
It had been changed so many times,
In each and every land.
The true meaning has been lost,
And by the time it came to the West,
Nobody could remember,
As the value became less than less.
Then along came competition,
Where it just had to look good,
Nice shapes, crisp and focused,
But empty, loud and awkward.
Before internet, video and books,
People learned using mnemonics,
Remembering with rhythm and cadence,
Kata had harmonics.
Tribes used to chant,
Then they would dance to a drum,
Learning was a social event,
Where the wizened would teach the young.
Health was always important,

So posture and breath were trained,
Along with mental intent,
The young became fully engaged.
Fighting moves were too simple,
More complex skills were desired,
Life was very active and diverse,
So a complexity of skills was required.
Battle and hunting was always with weapons,
It was rarely with bare hands,
So most of the moves were armed,
According to the weaponry of the lands.
If the warrior lost his weapon,
His opponent was still armed,
So his techniques had to be effective,
Against those that would cause great harm.
After World War Two in Japan,
Martial Arts were banned,
When Karate was finally allowed,
It was sport and empty hand.
So the reasons for kata are clear,
It is health skill and application,
Like a knot it has to be unraveled,
And studied with imagination.

Both Japanese and Chinese kata and forms contain three treasures:

1. Medical
2. Skill
3. Application

Medical comes first because you're most likely to die from ill health than any other cause, so it's the first line of self defence. We have to protect our mental, emotional and physical health. Before modern medicine, it was imperative to look after your own health therefore the right kind of exercise was necessary to maintain it. Our ancestors understood the importance of our life force and studied how it 'animated' our body. They realised the importance of posture, breath, mental clarity and the power of intention. Thus *kiai*, (*ki* = life force, *ai* = harmony) is to determine how this energy manifests itself in the body and how we enhance, channel and 'colour' or 'flavour' it, using our mind and intention. Many karateka think of it as a 'spirit shout' but of course it is much, much more than that.

The calligraphy for ki and chi is steam coming from a rice pot, rice being the staff of life, our food, plus the heat from activity, coupled with oxygen from the breath creates it. The energy runs with our intention and emotions, our blood, neurology, breath and activity, good postural integrity and no unnecessary tension keep the channels clear. The pumping action of feet to spine and core moves it rapidly inside an internal 'vacuum' of the pump, and the intention focuses and directs it. When you have internalised the qualities of kiai you become a person of *aiki* as in the art of aikido.

If you 'animate' you 'emanate'. As a consequence, this energy is sensed in a heightened fashion when anyone is in our personal space, thus we sense their state of aiki. A reason why 'soft skills' and our ability to present ourselves with a 'soft front and strong back' are so important is that because we emanate we can blend, harmonise and influence an opponent and their movement at this level.

If you think of energy healing like *reiki,* you can see how this can work. We have a brain because we move, its prime function is to anticipate (I go into this in more depth in my 'Soft Front, Strong Back' book)[1], so if both healer and healee's energies are in harmony, one to give healing and one to receive it, it can energise the healee's body to start healing itself. You can see how our energy is the 'driver' of the body—coloured with fear, it can lead to an involuntary retreat: this is why boxers stare each other out at the beginning of a fight. Where your mind and intention goes, your energy and body will follow.

Kata is a method of training this holistically. After explaining why it's important to have an opponent present when training, I also explain why they can't let that imaginary opponent win! Far too many do.

Skill training had to be 'compressed' into the the most efficient system, so all fighting techniques were reduced to the body principles that powered them, and then left and right and upper and lower body co-ordinations put together to be practiced in the optimum manner. The ability to manoeuvre the body applying these ideas and principles multi directionally and in spinning, turning, leaping and so forth also needed to be included. Kata is a 'knot' to be unravelled to find application. When studying any movement, it's important to be able to apply its source power to a myriad of techniques which usually include striking, receiving, locking, throwing, strangling and choking.

Finally all this knowledge had to be able to be applied to defend the practitioner, his family, village and country.

Different kata were invented for different purposes. When they were invented, many people couldn't read or write and were used

[1] Rowe, Steve: *Soft Front Strong Back*, 2023, The Ran Network
https://therannetwork.com/steve-rowe-soft-front-strong-back/

to receiving their skills and culture in dance, song and chants. It's easy to see how kata fits into these categories. Some were entire training systems in mnemonic, and some were training specific skill sets kinaesthetically.

It's also important to practice *ji yu* (freestyle) kata. I would often teach it from sparring in self defence style format, to being attacked by at least two attackers (usually four), so that as the defender was completing one defence, whatever position they were in, the next person would attack, then the next and so on. I would often sneak the attackers rubber knives, swords, baseball bats and plastic bottles, etc. to make the defender respond spontaneously; then the defender had a way of imagining the attackers to formulate their freestyle kata. There's not much point in practicing formulated kata if you don't move on to freestyle kata as well.

There's also a point to be made here that when we learn kata it's a bit like learning to draw by joining up the dots. The positions in a kata are not the kata, only a method of learning. We have to study every millimetre of movement: first there are the dots, then we join them up until there are no dots, then we colour it in to eventually paint a masterpiece. In the tai chi classics, they say that first we learn in feet, then inches, then hundredths of an inch then thousandths, then hundredths of a thousandth. If we have someone connected to our arms we realise that most of the good techniques are between the movements, and between the dots are all those applications previously mentioned.

It's often been asked why in a kata do we seem to do block after block, but in fact because the kata has two sides, if you just turn your head, it's an attack after attack. One side is evading and deflecting but the other side is attacking and striking. If one side is leaning away, the other side is leaning in. Toru always made the point that we were practicing two kata at the same time and in

Beside: Steve's wife Ann performing the perfect sidekick

case anyone was watching, we'd usually be looking to the defending side, consequently the onlooker wouldn't see the deadly techniques on the other side of the kata.

In the Wado Ryu training syllabus moves from kihon to *renraku waza* (combination techniques) allowing the build-up of the skills learned in kihon into fluid movement by combining them, still usually moving forward and backwards in straight lines into kata (forms), that vary the techniques and movements moving in all directions.

Wado Ryu originally had sixteen kata, starting with the five *Pinan* kata:

Pinan Shodan
Pinan Nidan
Pinan Sandan
Pinan Yondan
Pinan Godan

Pinan translates as the 'way of peace' or 'peaceful and calm' and are attributed to the Greatmaster Anko Itosu (1831 – 1915). Pinan Shodan, Nidan and Yondan lead to Ku Shan Ku and Sandan and Godan to Chinto.

The learning sequence continues then with:

Nai Han Chi
Ku Shan Ku
Sei Shan
Chinto

Nai Han Chi

Nai Han Chi means 'inner step progression' and the kata goes right back to the beginnings of martial arts in China. It includes stepping sideways and using internally rotated stances with whole body twisting and shaking techniques known as *fa jin* in Chinese kung fu. I'll write more about this later.

Ku Shan Ku

Ku Shan Ku kata was named after a Chinese Ambassador who was sent to Okinawa around 1756 and taught Kanga Sugasawa, who in turn devised the system kata in honour of his teacher. Along with Chinto, it is the main system kata of the Wado Ryu style.

Sei Shan

Sei Shan is a derivative of *San Chin*, which itself is a derivative of the Chinese *Sa'amchin* form, working in the 'dragon stepping', *yoko sei shan* (sideways sanchin stepping) in the first half, and *tate sei shan'* (forward sanchin) in the second half. A breakdown of the stances and techniques will follow later and I'll also write more about San Chin.

Chinto

Chinto is the other system kata and was named after a shipwrecked Chinese sailor stranded on Okinawa and forced to steal food to live. Matsumumara Sokon, a renowned karate master and King's bodyguard, was sent to defeat him, found himself equally matched and learned from him. This kata contains many snake and crane techniques. I remember failing my 3rd dan grading (I was quite good at failing gradings, proving the power of 'resolve' to get there in the end) by over enthusiastically doing the last spin in the kata and turning one and a half times instead of one, and ended up facing Toru sitting on the panel instead of away from him. He pushed his glasses up his nose (his way of showing annoyance) and waved for me to turn again, so I ended up facing the right way – it was at that moment I knew I'd failed.

These nine kata made up the teaching structure up to black belt and Toru maintained that they were all any karateka needed. Gichin Funakoshi, the founding father of Japanese karate, called Ku Shan Ku, Nai Han Chi, Sei Shan and Chinto the 'jewels in the crown' of karate.

The Pinans are derivative of the system kata Ku Shan Ku and Chinto, while Nai Han Chi trains the power sourcing required, and Sei Shan the internal system in the first half and the dynamic application in the second half.

Toru rarely taught the additional kata:
Passai
Wan Shu
Ro Hai
Ni Sei Shi
Jitte
Jion
Superinpei

Because of his studies of the brain and anatomy, Toru insisted on all techniques, kata and pairs work being practised equally on both sides, focusing on his codes, energetics and timings. His favourite kata was Pinan Yondan, as he felt that contained most of his teachings in a learnable way.

Because I was Chairman of the Governing Body for Karate in England, I often had to organise events. Once, when arranging the London Youth Games, I asked Toru if he would demonstrate a kata there. He refused. He told me to ask Keiji Tomiyama, as his kata 'was better'. Tomiyama's kata was certainly good but I knew there was another reason. When pushed, he said that he didn't like to demonstrate a kata all the way through in front of an audience, because they can 'see into your soul'. I didn't fully understand this at the time, but as the years have gone by, I now see that he was right. To do a kata well, you have go deeper than just technique, and like any real art, once you've made it your own, you reveal your innermost spirit, your soul.

CHAPTER NINE

How I Developed My Kata From Those Roots

Working in the security industry, I taught a lot of self defence. I taught security personnel of all types along with powers of arrest, search and questioning. I taught European presidential bodyguards, police and special services, then on home ground, rape crisis groups, milkmen, midwives, nurses, doctors on call, football pools collectors, insurance and debt collectors and the staff for many companies and gyms. To do this I had to build a training system that was effective for all genders and all ages. I started with elbow and knee strikes to teach how to fight close quarter, not be intimidated and to release power from the body. The elbow strikes went up, down, round and back and the knee strikes were front and angled. These could only be effective when the entire body was put into the strike and accelerated rapidly. To remember this I devised a simple 'close quarter form' consisting of these moves.

I then extended the elbow strikes out for a longer range with the same power sourcing into hand strikes using hammerfist, back-fist, palm heel and knife hand strikes. I put these into a simple form in the same order as the elbows and called it 'power hands'. The knee strikes I extended into stances and kicks and called it 'kicking form'. I took the four 'blocks' of karate and used them open hand to 'receive' the opponent's strikes, using the wedge and ball principles to either strike through or lock the opponent, and closed fist as strikes to the atemi points. I called this 'blocking form'. By this time, I had a lot of people calling for permanent classes and the system was proving so effective I was rolling the ideas into my karate classes.

Because I had been training in tai chi from the seventies, I had developed the ideas of 'soft front, strong back'. Tai chi had originally been called 'soft cotton boxing' and 'deceptive boxing', the idea being that the opponent would meet no resistance (like putting their hand into soft cotton) and the practitioner would meet, stick, follow and redirect their force leading them into 'nothingness'. Inside the soft cotton they would then find the 'sharp needle' of punishment. Using this I had developed a pushing hands system, utilising the four 'blocks' and taking *mawashi uke*, the circular block that applied the 'silk reeling' from tai chi, to roll around the arms of the opponent and apply a series of traps. I took mawashi uke and broke it down to its component parts of inward and outward circles and pull and push, to devise

a short form I called 'circles'.

To complete the system for those training long term in the dojo, I needed to add the internal mechanism and these kata were already in existence: therefore I added Sanchin (Sa'amchin), Tensho (Rokkusho) and Nai Han Chi (Naifunchin).

Sanchin (three battles)

Sanchin (Sa'amchin) = The resolution of the conflict between mind, body & breath.

Above: Sanchin

Sanchin is the internal training, the *neigong* and *qigong* of the martial Arts. It links the different level of breathing exercises to the different levels of physical co-ordination and mental awareness, sensitivity and intensity. It exercises the internal connection from feet to hands and the methods of utilising the spine and core for power.

It uses the three connected 'bows' of the body, the legs, spine and arms, to pump the energy and power around the body.

Many karateka use it for a more external 'dynamic tension' and forced valsavic style breathing, not realising that there's far more power using it for it's original purpose in deep internal training.

For those that are learning the kata or train it elsewhere, without this going into a huge deep unreadable treatise, let me list the fundamental considerations in a way that most people can understand to improve the form and give alternative ideas to the way you may already train:

- The 'Sanchin circle can be drawn around the outside of the feet.
- The diameter of the circle is the width of the shoulders.
- The head is the centre of the circle and should be 'suspended' from the crown – opening the occipital area.
- The 'plumb line' of the body should go from the crown of the head, down through the ear lobes, the centre of the shoulder, the centre of the hips to the arches of the feet.
- The tongue should lightly press to the top palate behind the front teeth.
- The ankle, knee and hip joints should be unlocked.
- The gentle outward spiral pressure of the feet to the floor should rotate the femur in the hip socket enough to open the inguinal crease in the hips. This alignment allows the bottom of the spine to drop, lengthening and loosening the spine.
- The chest should be sunk by 'letting go' and not forced inward.

The softening and connection of the core goes from the head through the neck, down through the myofascia in the chest around the heart and lungs, in to the diaphragm, through the psoas, inside the hips through the pelvic floor, down the inside of the legs, around the back of the knees, down the calves into the plantar fascia in the feet to the arches.

As previously explained, breathing is from the lower abdomen and back.

The 'Four pumps of chi' (ki) are the arches of the feet, the lower back, between the shoulder blades and the occipital area. These four pumps need to worked to manipulate the spine and core, and energise the breath, body and mind.

The first 'doughnut' of cells of any mammal go on to form the brain and spine, the core manipulates the spine and the vagus nerve that runs down the core controls the neurological web of the body, Sanchin trains the spine, core and vagus nerve together.

The positioning and movement of the body dictates the breathing method and this alters at each of the three levels of the form. The three levels of co-ordination are:

1. One side moves whilst the other is fixed.
2. Both sides move together powerfully manipulating the spine and core.
3. Both sides move in opposite directions and open and close sharply.

The 3 levels of breathing to match the co-ordination are:

1. First section - One breath followed by a half breath (to prevent dizziness)
2. Second section - Complete deep breaths using both abdomen and chest
3. Third section - Restrained breath control

The deep breathing from the lower abdomen and back draws the diaphragm down and fills the lungs fully with air. This puts more oxygen into the blood and brings it to the brain making the mind more aware. As already explained the qualities, in the mind are:

Awareness
Focus
Sensitivity
Intensity

It requires an aware and focused mind to utilise the sensitivity to read the body from the inside and increase the kinaesthesia (understanding where your body is in space and how it is aligned). The intensity is required to maintain that awareness, focus and sensitivity throughout the form.

The continuous good structure, aliveness and internal spiralling in the form maintains peng (ward off) and this can be tested by pressing against the practitioner in various places and differing angles. They should be able to resist without pushing back or leaning against the push. This is done by the internal spiral in the feet connecting to the core and out throughout the entire body.

Sanchin really has to be taught by a knowledgeable instructor who can correct and test each posture, but learned well, provides everything you need to know about the internal system that is lacking in most martial arts these days. It will also provide infinitely more power and function as a form of meditation and give vigorous health.

Tensho

Other names for Tensho are:

- Rokkishu
- Roku Six Hands
- Six Pivotal Skills
- Revolving Hands
- Heavenly Palms
- Spirit Hands
- Breathing Implicit In Ki
- Techniques Of Opportunity

I list all the names because they all have something to offer in understanding the kata. Chojun Miyagi created the Tensho kata by grafting the six hands of the five animal boxing system onto Sanchin.

The pivotal skills and revolving hands allow the practitioner to pass through and around the 'gates' of the opponents arms utilising the passing techniques of rolling around on the wrists, changing the hand shapes. The shamanistic aspects of the animals allow the practitioner to utilise the reptilian, mammalian and human aspects of the human brain and characteristics of the animals.

Application of Tensho kata

The five animals are:
- Snake
- Tiger
- Crane
- Dragon
- Leopard

The snake represents the way we move in curves. By pulsing to the floor, it coils around the opponent trapping, strangling and choking. It strikes quickly and venomously and represents our reptilian needs and nature that binds us to the earth.

The tiger is our bone and sinew strength, our warm blooded nature penetrating warrior gaze, leaping and ferociously ripping outward. It's our mammalian fearlessness and ferocity.

The crane steps quickly and lightly, flaps its wings fiercely, can peck, its wings fan like our fingers as we trap and turn our hands. It can fly to heaven representing our alchemy from the earthbound snake '*jing* energy' to our highest spiritual self '*shen* energy'.

The dragon is between snake and crane, the human representation of wisdom, the reptile that has wings and can fly to heaven in Western mythology. In the Asian mythology instead, dragons fly by magic, usually by clutching a pearl or a precious jewel and appear in many colours, representing the elements, and holding up the pillars of heaven. Rising and laying dragon techniques carry a lot of power and versatility.

The leopard represents speed and angular attacking. Unlike the tiger that relies on strength and power, it uses strategy, patience and intelligence: where the tiger rips outwards, the leopard rips inward. The leopard fist is a very versatile shape for both striking and ripping.

These techniques are used for:

Escapes
Traps
Strikes
Blocks
Chokes
Locks
Throws

A great addition to Sanchin to build skill level, with an incredibly versatile five animal boxing system.

Nai Han Chi

It is also called Naifunchin. I added this kata to include in the others *fajin*, another internally rotated stance powered by the three bows mentioned in Sanchin. Power comes from:

- Opening and closing the chest and back
- Twisting the waist against the hips
- Vibrating the hips connecting to the wrists
- Shaking power out of the entire body from feet to hands
- Pumping the three bows.

These three kata are the heart and soul of karate-do and my Shi Kon system.

CHAPTER TEN

The Structure of Uke

I was probably the first person in the UK to change the accepted meaning of the word uke in karate from 'block' to 'receive' and publish it in 'Traditional Karate' magazine. I was taking a private lesson in iaido in the Irish Working Man's Club in Dartford, across the road from Okimitsu Fuji's home. We were working on the form *uke nagashi,* where I would kneel down and he would approach me from the side and cut down to my head from *jodan no kamae* (sword raised above his head). My job was to rise up, deflecting his sword, move to his side and and cut cross from neck to hip. As I rose up I blocked his sword with a clash. "Uke!" he said, so we did it again….. and again, each time him saying "uke" a bit louder and me saying "hai Sensei!". Finally he said in an exasperated voice: "What do you think 'uke' means?" "block, Sensei" I replied.

"Ah, now I understand," he said, "it actually means 'to receive' or to 'invite in', the opposite to block." This was a revelation to me. I had also been doing some push hands work in both tai chi and *wing chun* at the time, and my friend Nathan Johnson had been working on a system that resembled the karate 'blocks'. This started me on a journey of 'uke' in karate, developing that 'soft front and strong back' and a push hands system utilising the four main uke, they being *uchi* (inner to outer), *soto* (outer to inner), *jodan* (upper) and *gedan* (lower), and developing my 'wedge and ball' theories.

If the hands are brought together into the 'praying' position ('child prays to Buddha' in kung fu, because an adult holds the incense sticks to their forehead, but a child holds them down to their chest so they can look around), this is the 'wedge' point (or *jeet* point in kung fu), and is the natural reach out and touch point at the edge of your personal space that you would meet the opponent. All contact with a skilled practitioner will be at this point. Toru appreciated this as he was against any wild swings of the limbs as appears in most karate styles. Whereas I would either wedge through to strike deflecting the opponent's attack at the same time, or turn the contact into a ball to deflect with a more tai chi type 'stick, follow, deflect and control', Toru would use the process outlined below.

in his writings, Toru translated 'uke' as 'to accept, catch or block" but understood that 'block' was misleading, and thus in the end settled on 'not to be hit'.

He gave three stages of uke (*Sen* means before, *Go* means after):

• *Go No Sen* - To 'block', to stop the opponent's attack and then attack back.
• *Sen No Sen* - To defend and attack at the same time, guarding yourself with one arm or leg without an actual block, but with firm contact to the opponent's attack.
• *Sen Sen No Sen* - To attack back against the opponent without any blocks, just guarding with the other arm without any contact to the opponent's attack.

He maintained that the best form of uke is not be near any confrontation or to run away, and it was only when you couldn't do this that you would have to employ the physical strategies.

Toru was incredibly scientific in his approach and in the books that we did together he would go to great lengths to explain Newtonian physics, Einstein's theory of relative motion and the fact that there was no fixed point in the universe. He also drew endless charts of the target areas, what parts of the limbs to use, against what technique, what position and therefore what type of 'uke' to use. We will address some of these as we go along but I am a very pragmatic person as I think most martial artists are and am primarily interested in how it's applied.

Toru applied this in a highly intelligent way in uke by not swinging the blocking arm and clashing with the opponent's attack but meeting it directly with a wedging motion and applying it with a counter movement of the body, and rotating it into the opponent with use of pivoting on the heel or ball of the foot.

For instance, with *shuto uke* (knife hand block) whereas most karateka would swing the arm around the body to clash with the opponent's arm, Toru would raise his arm directly to the contact point and use a counter movement of the body, turning it away from the arm to power the deflection. This way the arm directly covers the centre line of attack, there is no clash of arms, little strength is required to make it work and the body is taken out of line of the attack.

The same ideas are utilised in most of the other uke forms, emulating the 'rack and pinion' movement and works in the same way with uchi, soto, jodan and gedan uke's.

Soto and Uchi Uke (inner and outer receiving techniques)

There is confusion in Karate and indeed even with many Japanese as to which is which. Soto means 'out' or 'outer' and uchi means 'in' or 'inner'. The confusion arises as to how you look at it because the names apply to the opponent not the practitioner.

If the opponent raises both arms in front of him, everything receiving on the inside of the arms is 'uchi' and

Soto Uke

everything on the outside is 'soto'. So an inner to outer or outer to inner technique in the inside of his arms is uchi and on the outside is soto. Toru resolved this problem by referring to the practitioner and everything received on the thumb side of the arm moving outward was referred as *gaiwanto uke*' (*gai* means out) and everything received on the little finger side of the arm moving inwards was *naiwanto uke* (*nai* means in).

As karate was originally mainly grappling, the *hikite* (withdrawing) arm will be the disrupting arm, unbalancing the opponent so that the strike will be far more effective. There was originally no techniques involving just one arm. It was often referred to as 'husband and wife' hands with the receiving and disrupting hand being the 'feminine' wife hand and the punishing hand being seen as the 'male' and 'husband' hand.

Tai Sabaki (Body Evasion Skills)

So far we have talked about meeting and receiving the attacks from the opponent, but the greatest skill is to not be there to receive it. *Tai sabaki* is the skill to move the body out of the way of the attack. This can be done unskilfully by running away or making large 'panic' movements that enable the attacker to continue their attack from a position of strength, or you can use skill. Further on it this book I will

Above: Shuto Uke. Previous page: Hikite.

explain in detail the ways and codes that Toru taught to move the body quickly and effectively. These can be utilised to move around the opponent's attack and close the distance.

One of those skills is in the second part of the story I told earlier about my iaido lesson with Okimitsu Fuji. The technique, if you remember, was uke nagashi; he described nagashi as a stone placed in a river and the water running around it to meet at the other side. The ability to move the feet only around ten degrees or so to change angle and 'slip' the opponents technique, whilst also turning inwards and moving forward to strike, lock or throw at the same time is the highest skill. This can be done soto (outside) or uchi (inside) the opponent's attack.

Toru used to tell the story of watching the Grandmaster and founder of the Wado Ryu style of karate Hironori Ohtsuka, who was also a master of ju jitsu and was in his seventies, move effortlessly around his opponents and deliver his techniques without any force, strength or competitive force required.

CHAPTER ELEVEN
The Structure of Tachi Kata
(Stance Work)

Toru taught that is was absolutely essential to learn how to adopt and use the stances in karate, training correctly, for the following reasons:

- To be able to execute techniques, obtaining the maximum effect from the skills outlined in this book
- To get co-ordination between upper and lower and left and right spheres of the body
- To maintain balance
- To strengthen the legs
- To take positions natural to the body
- To achieve free and nimble movement in all directions

To do this we need to be able:

- To position the feet with regard to the direction and angle of the body
- To have the correct distance between the feet with regard to stance length and width
- To bend the knee joints to the optimum angle
- To correctly position the body with regard to weighting the front, back or both legs
- To measure the stance length and width according to body size.

Correct stances are important for joint safety and structure. If the knees bend too far the stance collapses; if the the stance is too long or too wide, the body-weight can't go squarely in the feet and being 'sprawled' makes one unstable, immobile and unable to move effectively or repel the opponents force. To be honest, I've rarely met a karateka with good stance work. When asked which leg they have their weight in, most give the wrong leg because they're unable to weight the correct leg: either their stance is too long/wide, or they're 'on their legs' and not 'in them', unable to soften into and access the legs properly to release their body-weight. This means not to realise the importance of the chest, waist, pelvic floor and femoral triangle in connecting the upper and lower body.

The spiralling in the feet also plays an important role. Getting into a stance involves spiralling both feet in the same direction until the stance needs to be flexed to apply the technique, and then they spiral in opposite directions engaging the four myofascial chains in each leg (front, sides and back), without affecting the joints and opening the hips. This enables the pelvic floor to be lifted and the pubococcygeus muscle to be engaged, in turn enabling the spine to be bowed and all the deeper muscles of the body to be utilised for internal power.

If the legs are not spiralled, they won't flex in the stance, using

only the front and back myofascial lines. This makes them unstable and unable to open the hips and connect to the spine. The spine has three bows for mobility, the lower back, in between the shoulder blades and the occipital; being able to release and bow them means that the chest and lower abdomen can also function properly.

I discussed the Sanchin kata earlier, but the 'sanchin circle' around the feet still apply in all stances around the weighted leg, with the other leg outside the circle to support it. If you study this it really helps to understand how to weight the leg properly.

Many karateka think that they have to sacrifice mobility for stability, not understanding that one feeds the other. If we are well balanced, we are stable and the flexing of momentary stability as a technique is applied feeds the pump for continuous mobility. Movement is fed by a succession of pulses of stability/mobility in balance.

As I said earlier, kamae is an interesting Japanese word that involves the whole body position and more importantly is adopting an 'attitude' that includes intention and spirit.

CHAPTER TWELVE

Makiwara Training

Maki means to wind around and *wara* 'rice straws'. You make rope with the rice straws and then wind it around the post with padding underneath to make a *makiwara*. Toru was taught that the rice straw rope prevented infection in the fists when they bleed and he claimed that he found this to be true as he never got infection or needed medication. Rice straw was abundant and inexpensive in Japan.

I used a makiwara daily for over 40 years and never had injury or callouses on my knuckles. I found it a useful training tool being rooted at ground level like a human being and with the right amount of 'give' and 'spring' I could test my alignment, focus and ability to absorb and ground recoil energy. Injury and callouses are the result of bad technique and the knuckles slipping on impact.

The makiwara should ideally be treated cedar the same height as you. Five inches square at the bottom tapering to five by two inches at the top. When buried, it should be chest height and bound as described above. The traditional way is to put large stones around the base of the makiwara in the hole, gradually adding smaller and smaller stones until you get the yield that you want. People often use concrete with iron bars in to stabilise the concrete and diffuse the energy so it doesn't crack.

The best way to use the makiwara is to start with reverse punches (*gyakuzuki*) stepping into the punch to utilise the acceleration, body weight and twist, timing the punch to land with the step and carry the weight and power into the punch. This should be practised both sides and followed by lead hand jab (*tobikommizuki*), back fist (*uraken*), hammer fist (*tettsui*), palm heel (*teisho*), knife hand (*shuto*) and ridge hand (*haito*). You can also practice your *keri* (kicks) on the makiwara.

Many years ago I wrote a poem about makiwara training in karate. It is entitled 'Blood On Wood':

Blood On Wood
Thump, thump, thump…
He's out there again,
Hitting that bloody piece of wood in the garden,
One of those Kung Fu nutters.
Every bloody day it's the same,
Well I ain't gonna tell him,
He'll probably tie me up like a pretzel,
And post me back through our letterbox.
Thump, thump, thump,
Each time strike with seiken,
Shuto, tettsui and teisho,
Haito, koken and nukite.
Feet press directionally to the floor,
Spiraling through the legs,
Connecting through the core,
And powering out through the hands.
Thump, thump, thump,
The makiwara bends and is momentarily held,
The return force is repulsed,
Creating a 'double tap' of energy.
Thump thump thump,
Every day is a penny in the martial arts bank,
The blood on the wood is a reminder,
That everyone bleeds,
And all matter is impermanent.
Thump, thump, thump,
While life goes on we evolve,
Our resolve determination and courage,
Patience kindness and compassion,
Make us true martial art warriors…
One day there will be silence…

The makiwara will grow moss,
Nature will take it's course,
As all things pass…

It shows the deep relationship that a karateka forms with the makiwara over the years. Mine was always in my garden and though the neighbours often mentioned me striking it and the resulting vibrations, they never complained.

CHAPTER THIRTEEN

TN 1,2,3

TN stands for *tobikomi-zuki* (stepping front jab punch) and *nagashi-zuki* (angled simultaneous avoid and punch)

Toru was always telling me off for studying Buddhism, Zen, Taoism and other meditation practices and insisted that I study science, physiology and the human brain. As stated before, Toru used the 'hook technique' of computer operation, where you can press one button and a whole screen of information would be hooked up to it. He used code numbers as the key and attached the necessary information to each code.

Because the brain had two sides, the left side of the brain controls the right side of the body and the right controls the left. Consequently, Toru would make sure that we learned every technique and form equally on both sides.

He asked us to 'computerise' the brain using his codes, so that eventually when the skills were internalised, no thought would be required and the body would react automatically.

For tobikomi-zuki and nagashi-zuki skills, he used their first letters 'TN' as in TN1, TN2 and TN3.

- TN1 is to project the body weight forward from the back foot.
- TN2 is bring the back foot forward quickly without dragging (TN2D) or hanging (TN2H).
- TN3 is TN1 + TN2 backwards.

We move forward, backward, sideways and in a combination of these angles. The key is to always move both feet in the above fashion and that way the body weight moves efficiently and you're never 'sprawled' immobile or awkwardly in a stance; on the contrary, you are able to keep moving.

Similar footwork is used in kendo (*suriashi*) and boxing. It's good to remember that the angle of the feet also dictate the angle of the body.

Previous page: Tobikomi-zuki

CHAPTER FOURTEEN

The Structure Of 'Keri'

(Leg Techniques)

Most kicking techniques in karate along with many other martial arts were introduced by the French from their art of savate, along with formation training and non/semi contact competition. When you look at the old kata and other old martial arts, there were only low target 'leg manipulations', like manipulating the opponent's knees, treading or stamping on their legs or sweeping, trips and throws. High kicks and circular spinning kicks were introduced by Gichin Funakoshi's son Yoshitaka, who - according to researcher and practitioner Donn F. Draeger - transformed Shotokan karate between 1936 and 1945.

This led to the more flamboyant form of karate with longer stances, bigger movements, higher, jumping and spinning kicks, non-contact sport karate and a sport that was visually more exciting if not as effective as the the older Okinawan form.

As a language expert, Toru always thought that the translation of keri to 'kick' was a bad one. He believed that was the cause of a lot of bad techniques and injuries because he maintained that 'kick' to an Englishman was the motion of the leg to kick a football or a tin can down the road. He said that 'keri' was all motions that could be done by the legs for an attack. It included the swing motion but also includes a thrusting or stamping movement. There are two possible pivot points in keri, the hip and the knee. Toru was very conscious of joint safety and thought it important to protect both joints with the techniques.

Because 'kick' is a common translation, for the reader's understanding I will use it at times for convenience (although I can feel Toru frowning).

Toru differentiated leg techniques into 'swing' and 'thrust' motions and pointed out that an attack using keri involved standing on one leg, leaving the practitioner open to attack and therefore it had to be performed quickly and efficiently. Despite his natural flexibility, he was not an advocate of high or spinning kicks. One of his favourite expressions was "to kick to the head is about as efficient as trying to punch someone in the foot."

With his unique mind and understanding of Einstein's theories, he was able to view the different leg techniques without the limitation of environment. This meant that he was able to see how the skills required related to each other at different angles. He saw that all the different techniques required the placing of the supporting foot to give distance, angle, body line and power. They all required the knee to be raised and returned to the same point, and in extension the required joint safety had to be observed and to return without being grabbed. Accordingly, he devised a set of codes that has stood me in good stead for all kicks for over 40 years.

He split the code into four parts and then each part into its constituent parts. The first one was 'K1', where 'K' stands for keri.

K1

Take the ball of the foot off the floor and keep raising it. This avoids delay. If you raise the heel first (as most people do), the force goes down to the floor and comes back up again taking up unnecessary time. It also makes the head 'nod' forward giving the technique away. You have to keep raising it to prevent it from swinging out and injuring yourself on the opponent and to enable it to take a straight line to the target.

K2

K2 consists of two parts, to raise the knee as high as you can, chambering it nice and tight, before swinging, snapping or thrusting to prevent the foot from swinging out and upwards and to get that straight line to the target; and to then quickly return it to the same position to defend and be able to kick again if needed.

K3

K3 is to snap or thrust without fully extending the leg as to do so will slow the kick down, making it easier to grab. The angle also changes in the last part of the movement modifying the trajectory, something that can cause serious knee damage.

K4

K4 has three parts. The first is to move the supporting foot between K1 and K2 to get into position quickly and avoid damage to the knee of the supporting leg. Then to not move the foot from the knee raise through the leg extension and the return to the chamber: this way you remain stable and don't slow down due to unnecessary movement. The third part is to keep the supporting leg bent as much as possible throughout the entire technique to prevent knee damage to it, to improve the quality, power and body line of the technique and enable you to move forward or back with the TN skills explained earlier.

Toru made the point that it takes time and practice to internalise these skills and join them up to develop fluidity and gain their benefit.

There was criticisms that this method of coding created 'clockwork' form of 'karate by numbers', and to be honest, with some practitioners who never joined the skills up to get that fluidity, the criticism was valid, but it was not Toru's intention to do that, only a lack of understanding by some. You only had to see Toru in action to understand!

Let's look at some examples of how they're used in basic leg techniques.

Mae Geri (Front Kick)

Adopt left guard, turn the left foot slightly out without creating friction by taking the sole very slightly off the floor, and at the same time take the ball of the right foot directly off the floor.

This skill drastically reduces the kicking time. Most people will instead move the front foot first, often pivoting with frictional loss on the floor. They will then lift the heel of the kicking leg, pushing the upper body forward, thus giving it away to the opponent and having to use a push and then pull motion, reducing three motions to just one.

It also changes the muscle usage from calf to quadriceps and instead of your upper body movement being towards the opponent, it moves backward for balance and is not read as a threat.

Raise the knee as high as possible with the leg tightly chambered, with the ball of the foot pointing directly towards

the target: this is protective, as it enables you to kick if the opponent moves forwards and prevents you from injuring your foot, ankle or shin with an upward swing.

Snap the shin forward without straightening the leg fully (to prevent knee damage and that 'upward swing' that would take place as you fully extend changing the direction of the technique), and stretch the

Mae Geri K2

Mae Geri K3

ankle so that the sole of the foot travels parallel to the ground and the ball of the foot hits the opponent in a straight line, snapping it back to the chambered position.

This allows you to kick again if necessary and prevents the opponent from moving forward. It also means that you are able to withdraw, move forward or at any angle.

Move from this chambered position by bending the supporting leg as this enables the TN1,2 and 3 skills to be employed moving directionally, rather than falling forward in an uncontrolled way.

Mawashi Geri (Round Kick)

Mawashi means 'round' and Toru taught the old-fashioned angled variation of mae geri, still kicking with the ball of the foot. He didn't teach the more popular 'sport' version striking with the instep or the full hip twist version to clear the shoulder and get to the head. As I stated earlier, he wasn't a fan of head kick.

Sokuto Geri (Foot Knife Kick)

Sokutu literally means 'foot knife', describing the outer edge of the foot. In many styles this technique is called *yoko geri*, meaning 'side kick'. The confusion in translating is that a side kick could mean a front kick done to the side.

In basic training it can be practiced to the side but is often done to the front. Applying the codes, the supporting foot is taken directly to the finished position, with the leg bent as much as possible for power and support, and the heel pointing toward the target. At the same time the sole of the kicking leg has to be taken directly off the floor, chambering the leg to the knee-high position with the leg 'cocked' and foot facing the target.

Sokuto geri

This kick is a 'thrust' kick from the hip, striking with the blade of the foot at the heel, and taking care to use the correct angle so as to not pivot with the knee: this would make it change angle into a 'round kick'. Do not fully extend the leg and return it immediately to the chambered position, bending the supporting leg to enable TN 1,2, and 3, to move parallel to the floor after the technique.

Ushiro Geri

Ushiro means 'back or 'rear'. Ushiro geri is a thrusting movement like sokuto geri, but to the rear.

I remember when we were teaching in Norway that a visiting

4th Dan karateka was saying to Toru how slow a back kick to the front was compared to others. Toru bet him that I could do a back kick faster than he could do a front kick, because his codes made all the kicks the same speed. He was to drop a handkerchief and when it touched the floor we had to both kick at the same time, and sure enough, I was faster.

It's hard sometimes to appreciate his genius because the codes mean that speed is a result of the developed skill and therefore didn't necessarily feel or look faster. The science, however, meant that it was and I have used this technique to devastating effect particularly toward an attacking opponent, sometimes lifting them right off the floor.

I remember Toru asking the students on a seminar what was so special about this kick, and no one could answer. He demonstrated it on his uke and ran out the

Ushiro geri

hall. We all waited for a couple of minutes wondering where he had gone, when his face appeared round the door with a cheeky grin saying: "you can kick and run away!"

CHAPTER FIFTEEN

Kumite

(Grappling Hands or Sparring)

Ippon (one step) Sanbon (three step) and Gohon (five step) Sparring

These are a very basic form of pairs work with an attacker moving forward one, three or five times with either *junzuki* (step and punch) or *maegeri* (step through with front kick), and the defender stepping back in harmony with 'blocking' techniques and on the last step responding with a counterattack. Any of the blocking techniques can be used and the counter can vary from a reverse punch to any attacking manoeuvre. Toru only taught the one step as he couldn't really see the point of the three or five steps.

Learning to retreat yet remain powerful is a skill in itself: it's surprising how many people stumble and trip when moving backwards in a fight. You only have to look at street fights on YouTube or social media to see how the defender tends to over balance. Once the students got used to retreating I changed it to a half step backwards and forwards with the same defence so they changed sides on the spot. When they were familiar with that, I changed it again so they stepped forward with the same defence into the attack deflecting and countering in one movement. This aligned with go no sen, sen no sen and sen sen no sen.

Ohyo Kumite

Ohyo kumite was invented by Tatsuo Suzuki in Wado Ryu and means 'practical application'. It was designed to bridge the gap between the more formal pairs work and free sparring, thus it included more mobile fighting techniques with sweeps and throws. This is good mobility training with varying techniques and useful for learning competition strategies.

Previous page: Ohyo Kumite

Kihon Kumite

Hironori Ohtsuka originally registered thirty-six *kihon kumite* but bought them down to ten. These contain the classic budo roots of Wado Ryu from Shindo Yoshin Ryu Ju Jitsu and show the advanced ideology contained in the style. Consideration is given to:

- **Maai**
  Maai is good judgement of the fighting distance between opponents to maximise manoeuvrability and gain strategic advantage. You can see the constant adjustment at the beginning of each kihon kumite.
- **Zanshin**
  Zanshin translates as 'remaining mind', meaning that a continuous awareness is maintained all of the time: in kihon kumite that is from the bow at the beginning to the bow at the end. The heightened and changing awareness plays an important part in the kihon kumite. You can liken it to the 'traffic light system' that many self defence teachers employ.
- **Tai Sabaki**
  As I've already said, tai sabaki is an essential aspect of Wado Ryu and can clearly be seen in each one of these ten kumite. It should be noted that the root word sabaki has the concept of 'just enough' or 'optimum utilisation'. A notable part of the Wado Ryu style is that all movements are practised efficiently with no wasted motion.
- **Sen Sen No Sen, Sen No Sen and Go No Sen**
  We have already explained but needs to be listed here as one of the essential strategies.
- **Nagasu**
  Nagasu is the same as nagashi.
- **Inasu**
  Inasu is to dodge or deflect, ducking and moving inside, or

around an attackers technique.

- **Noru**

  Noru is to "ride" moving in contact with the opponent's technique. This is similar to the 'stick, follow and redirect' of tai chi.

- **Irimi**

  Irimi is to get inside an opponents technique to create an opening.

- **San-mi-Ittai**

  San-mi-Ittai are three kinds of movement exemplified in the kihon kumite.

  - *Ten-I*, to move away from the attack.

  - *Ten-tai*, to realign the body changing the angle to attack and reduce the exposed target area.

  - *Ten-gi*, executing techniques while letting the attack pass through.

Kihon Kumite

- **Ki Ken Tai no Ichi**

  The co-ordination of the mind and body combined with good technique.

- **Hei Jo Shin**

  Hei Jo shi translates as 'keep your usual mind', meaning your cultured, calm, still, aware and powerful mind. I have this calligraphy on my dojo wall drawn by a zen master and bought back from Japan by Okimitsu Fuji as a present.

- **Randori (free fighting)**

  The rules for free fighting can vary from association to

association, club to club and tournament to tournament and of course have changed over time in most places. In Okinawa in small family run clubs they would wear *bogu*, a kendo style armour for full contact, to test techniques. The armour was developed for *shobu ippon* and *sanbon kumite* competitions (one-point and three-point competition). Originally, in shobu ippon competition no protection was worn and the criteria for the winning point was *ikken hissatsu*, meaning 'to annihilate with one blow', with exquisite control but still quite hard contact. Over time, rules were extended to many different clubs, associations and governing bodies, and to make it more visual different rules with a varying number of points were introduced for mid level and head strikes and kicks. The Kyokushinkai style developed 'knockdown' tournaments, where a competitor wins by knocking the opponent down to the floor calling, themselves the 'hardest' style of karate.

I attended the Kyokushinkai 'knockdown' tournaments for many years and the founder of the style in the UK, Steve Arniel, became a good friend. In my opinion, they were the most visually engaging. To fight in the later rounds, the competitors also had to break a number of one inch thick piranha pine boards, with top competitors often breaking up to five boards. The breaking demonstrations of baseball bats and blocks of ice were also very exciting. I made many good long term friends in their association.

The 'non contact' and 'semi contact' tournaments never appealed to me. When I started Shi Kon, we had a strong tournament team thanks to Ian Cuthbert and Geoff Thompson (multi talented World Champion) and I admire the top competitors in any of the karate sports, but my interests were elsewhere. I'd done too much fighting in the street, working in the security trade, and full contact without armour in my early training days, so I found no joy in any forms of competition. I only competed when asked to by Toru and I also qualified as a governing body referee when asked, but never wanted to do that either. On social media, I avoid the martial art 'street' and *bunkai* (they should really say 'ohyo', as it's application) videos and never comment or share them, as to be honest, most wouldn't work against a really violent attacker.

When the Berlin wall came down and in Germany and Czechoslovakia they had their 'velvet' revolution, I travelled to the first Czech international tournament hosted by Ondra Musil. Our team won most of the medals and Ondra asked if I'd do seminars for them. Unbeknown to me, the only people that had been able to train under Russian occupation were the President's bodyguards, their special services and police self defence instructors, who made up the participants on my first seminar! Luckily that was right up my street. They had previously been travelling to Germany to train under a Japanese Shotokan instructor but my material was more suited for their needs. Shi Kon Czechoslovakia was formed and I've continued that relationship for what is now around 33 years, introducing them to Wado Ryu karatedo, iaido, aikido and tai chi. Many of those first participants still train with me. Our annual summer camps in Jizerka have been running for all that time and now are mainly tai chi and aikido.

I taught in Norway originally with Toru. When we split, some students continued with me and I taught there for around sixteen years, spreading to Denmark, Sweden, Ireland and Portugal.

These days, due to old age and health, I can't travel as much, so I only teach in the Czech Republic when I can and their instructors travel to me.

CHAPTER SIXTEEN

Why I Gave Up Politics In Karate

In the eighties I held many positions in the Governing Bodies of Karate. I sat on the executive committee, was the secretary, the chairman and represented karate on the Martial Arts Commission. I naively went into politics assuming that I could work for the good of karate. I expected all the senior grades to be the same, living exponents of the philosophy that underlies the art. I couldn't have been more wrong. It was like the politics that you find in our own government at the moment. It was an oligarchy built around power and money.

A governing body needs to do more than just arrange tournaments, it needs look after a unified membership, the standard of karate, arrange pathways to excellence, administration for the clubs, insurance, coaching qualifications, health and safety and maintain standards. It needs to be as inclusive as possible. In relation to tournaments, it needs to look after those pathways for prospective top-level competitors, their training, fair selection, seeded tournaments, referee training and qualification, extra insurance for competitors, record all injuries and disqualifications to be able to put the most successful national and international teams together.

And guess what? It was riven with political splits, rivalry and egos. At that time virtually nothing was done for the membership and everything went towards the broken tournament structure. At the time the magazines were very tournament oriented and I remember being told at a committee meeting that 'tournament is the shop window of karate'.

Nothing could be further from the truth. Those of us on the ground knew that people joined our clubs because:
- They had watched a Bruce Lee movie or the 'Kung Fu' series on TV.
- They wanted to get fit.
- They wanted to be able to defend themselves.
- They wanted to get out and socialise.

Even for the competitors, there was no defined routes to

excellence, no seeded competitions; a beginner could fight a world champion in their first tournament fight. No competitors licences were issued giving additional insurance, record of wins, injuries, penalties and disqualifications and top level competitors tended to come from just a few instructors.

I tried many times to explain to the committee of 'governing by consent' and that we needed to provide a service to everyone paying fees and find 'the highest common denominator' to keep everyone in the tent pissing out and not have too many outside pissing in, but it fell on deaf ears. They continuously tried governing by intimidation and bullying anyone on the outside using any income for their officials, and as a consequence they continuously had to deal with breakaway groups and others not registering in the first place. It was doomed from the start.

It was at this point that I decided to start writing to change the perspective and give out information that would not otherwise be available. I started submitting articles to Combat magazine edited by Bey Logan and then Traditional Karate magazine when it started. I wrote on what I felt was important to normal karateka: at one point I was writing quite a bit of the content with the following columns:

The Steve Rowe Column
Voice From The Deep
Business File
Coaching Corner

I also did several interviews with other well known martial artists.

At that time columns were still being written on one of the first Amstrad computers and photos were being taken on film, so we had to take and develop loads of photos and hope we had some good ones! The printed article and developed photos had to then be submitted by post.

By this time I had formed Shi Kon and it had grown to be a large association with around fifteen thousand members. Much of the success was due to my views voiced in my magazine columns and seminars. That gave me a substantial voting block in the governing body and therefore influence.

The only other 'traditional' karateka around in politics at that time was Chris Rowen, who'd just got back from living in Japan and studying with Goju Kai founder Gogen Yamaguchi. I sponsored Chris's membership to the governing body and we became firm friends. Chris became the Secretary and we ran the office out of his dojo in Old Street in London. As a Shinto priest, over the years Chris has cared for my dojo shrine and taught on many of my seminars. His versions of Sanchin and Tensho have had influence on my understanding. We are still good friends.

Around that time there was a major split in the Governing Body with a lot of enmity. As Chairman of the English Karate Council, I started the negotiations with the English Karate Board simply because I felt that we could achieve so much more as a cohesive body. Eventually it came about and the English Karate Governing Body was formed with the support of Sport England. It started well and with Sport England's support we managed to get a full time office, put together a nationally recognised National Vocational Qualification structure. Then rivalry, enmity, greed and corruption once gain took over and I resigned, luckily long before it collapsed in 2006 with a million pounds missing!

By that time, I'd moved over to Martial Arts Illustrated magazine and around the millennium conducted many interviews with all the senior EKGB members and committee with the EKGB Column and also had my 'Beyond Technique' column.

As the EKGB collapsed, there was no governing body left to continue with all the good work but luckily with my tai chi studies I managed to join the British Council For Chinese Martial Arts and also register my own art as Shi Kon Kung Fu. This meant we could continue with our NVQ coaching centre and get the prestigious Sport England 'Clubmark' accreditation. I and all my members became lost to the karate world.

CHAPTER SEVENTEEN
How I Formed My Own System

At that time I reviewed all my training and teaching structures. I decided that being well into my fifties I still had a lot of personal progress to make and time was getting short. That was when I chose to drop all the Wado kata apart from Naihanchi and focus on the Shi Kon kata and Sanchin, Tensho and Naihanchi. As most beginners joined for health and self defence, to fulfil their expectations when they joined the club I added kickboxing. We had an active start with a lot of pad work and exercise, that gave two ways of joining the dojo: the active fitness route of self defence with kung fu (was karate), that eventually led to the deeper methods of training; or tai chi, that started softly with meditation (neigong) and energy exercises (qigong), coupled with tai chi form and push hands that eventually led to the martial with the Yang Family Kung fu and weaponry. Both routes started at opposite ends of the spectrum but ended up in the same place. Two paths up the mountain but when you get to the top, the view is the same.

I did this against all advice. My wife and many students and instructors loved the white karate suits, the regimen of the traditional Japanese way of line training, the Japanese terminology and were telling me that I would lose all my students. However, I knew that we were moving more towards gym culture with a meditative aspect by changing the uniform to the more comfortable T shirt, by teaching in plain English and making lessons more friendly but hard working. I chose a 'workshop' type atmosphere, focusing on what was important in learning rather than uncomfortable clothing and foreign language: it was the way of the future. And I was right, as we gained students instead of losing them.

This enabled me to focus on the tai chi. In Zen they say 'enter a small door but penetrate deeply': I instinctively knew which way I had to go and what I needed to learn. My progress accelerated rapidly and I'm still training twice a day, studying and writing, despite all my health problems, at 73 years old. Mindful training and study coupled with insight meditation from my Buddhist roots and Toru's method of keywords and principles has paid off in spades with my martial arts studies.

CHAPTER EIGHTEEN

The Learning Process

An oft quoted phrase in Japanese is '*shu ha ri*', that translates as 'first learn, then detach and finally transcend'. It's giving us advice on how to use the structure to learn.

'First learn' means to internalise the ideas, principles, philosophy and techniques of your art and style. Most people quote the phrase as an excuse to break away from their existing group but that's not what it means. Internalisation takes its time, depending on the depth of the system; most traditional styles will take about twenty years of daily study, but that's only a guideline.

Once internalised, 'ha' means to adapt what you've learned to suit your way better but still be right. You should be able to explain the ideas, principles and techniques in your own way and in your own words and still be right.

'Ri' means that you've absorbed and internalised the system and adaptions so well that whatever you do will be right as you couldn't do it in any other way. You're totally free of the system! You've made the complete move from someone who does martial arts to being a martial artist. If you were cut in half, it would have 'martial artist' written all the way through you like a stick of rock!

Like any art, it's not what you do but the way that you do it that counts. It's easy to be a technician but you have to be able to 'release your soul' to be an artist. I know many good technicians in the martial arts, music and arts that are good at what they do but they have no soul in it. I remember discussing an excellent iaido technician with Okimitsu Fuji and he said "yes, he's good, too good". I asked how someone could be 'too good' and he replied: "You need a bit of 'pirate' in you, otherwise you're only a soulless technician". I understood what he meant.

Being a good student

We often talk about what makes a good instructor and what makes a good club, but what happens when we turn that on its head and ask what makes a good student?

The one thing that I discovered was that if I knew how to be a good student, I could get far more out of my instructors than anybody else, and that as an instructor I am far more inclined to teach a good student thoroughly than a bad one.

The inescapable facts are that many instructors don't get to choose their students. Sometimes they teach because they feel it's wrong to favour students and therefore 'stick it out' with what they consider a bad one, as Toru did with me in the beginning. Sometimes the reasons are financial, but either way I quickly discovered that there are ways to get far more than anyone else was getting and I didn't have to compromise my morals to achieve it!

You don't have to like a person to teach them well, a student doesn't have to like an instructor to learn from them, all it takes is a bit of patience and tolerance on both sides to get there. I've had a love/hate relationship with many students in the past and I can understand that they hate me for being blunt with them and for making them do things that they didn't want to. If you don't push them beyond what they think are their limits, how are they going to improve? If they don't have that basic faith and trust in me even if they don't like me or what I'm making them do, they can never grow as a martial artist. I never worried about popularity, just results.

What can a student do to make the relationship work better? This is the magic formula that I used to get that extra tuition and information that the others never got.

Always pay your fees. Seems obvious but isn't to many. Never barter on a price. Always pay for your lesson whether you turn up or not. If you want that regular spot, book it with money, then it's always yours and a bond of trust is formed. There is nothing worse than a student that books an instructor's time, cancels and doesn't pay. If someone who does pay regularly comes along, they will

naturally give the time to them, and you will forfeit yours. The instructor will also not be inclined to teach an irregular person well because they will see them as untrustworthy and think that they are wasting their time. If you are a long-term student, raise the fees yourself, it is unlikely that the instructor will do it and when you show that you value their time and consider their well-being, it will be appreciated.

Always make notes. Learn a training shorthand of matchstick men, arrows and keywords, so that when you get home you will remember what you've been taught. Ask the instructor to film you doing what you've just learned on your phone and if you're lucky he will give advice whilst doing it. If he doesn't want to do this get someone else to do it as soon as possible afterwards. Between lessons train continuously on what you've been taught and think about it all of the time. Every time a question arises, write it down to ask on your next lesson. There's nothing more encouraging for an instructor than a student who pays attention, makes notes, trains hard between lessons and then asks questions on the next lesson.

Listen and pay attention to what you're being taught. Don't give your opinion. Don't talk about what you've done or what you think, because you're paying the instructor to give you the benefit of their experience. There's nothing more boring than a student who pays the instructor so they can talk to them for a couple of hours about what they think and have done. Every minute is important and not just from a financial point of view: that instructor could be dead tomorrow and you're wasting precious time with your own ego. If you're asked: "What do you want to do?", the instructor is being polite. Answer: "Whatever you think I need to work on". You are likely being taught a system and it's best to learn it in the right sequence put together by the expert, not randomly by your own desires.

Develop respect and care. If the Instructor is doing their best for you and you are for them, mutual respect is earned naturally. If there's anything you can do to help or support in their home life, club and association development, do it, because it means that your teaching environment is less likely to be affected by outside influences and it's good to care. Don't forget that I've represented my instructors on Governing Body Committees, helped them to write books, shoot videos, buy houses, helped with legal problems, opened clubs for them, taught on their seminars and helped them bring over their instructors to the UK.

Every time you reach a milestone in your training, like a grading, winning a tournament or opening your own club, always thank your instructor before doing anything else, and always give them credit for what they've taught you. Nowadays that courtesy has all but disappeared and you can see students prancing around with their new grade or trophy and everyone patting them on their back, whilst the instructor sits quietly in the corner. It's not inappropriate to buy them a small thank you gift or at least give a thank you before celebrating yourself. Fuji would always send me to a grading with the instruction "if you fail don't come back" (I think he was joking). When I returned, I would always give him a small gift that he would place on his shrine unopened and clap his hands to wake the gods.

It's easy to teach just the surface of a system and the student would never know. Often that's done as a test to see if they're worthy or capable of receiving deeper instruction. Courtesy is a given, respect is earned both ways. When the student and instructors 'ki is in agreement', respect has been earned and they are capable of working through the hard times together; the 'hidden levels' can be taught. Nothing is being held back, it's just that the environment has to be right. The surface teaching is known as 'eating sweet' and the deeper levels as 'eating bitter'. 'Eating sweet' is full of flashy moves and certificates and 'eating bitter' is made of sweat, blood, pain and a system that gradually alters the body and mind.

By all means find the right club and instructor, but remember that they are also looking for the right student.

CHAPTER NINETEEN

Grading

Gradings are always a controversial subject and social media is littered with endless emotive arguments about which way and to what standards people grade. Whenever I put this poem on social media it gets thousands of shares and engagement.

> *I used to think everyone could be a black belt.*
> *The 'way' was simple;*
> *All they had to do was train every day for 3 – 5 yrs,*
> *Attend 2 or 3 lessons a week,*
> *Pay attention to instruction,*
> *And they would make the grade.*
> *Over the years I realised that was not true.*
> *Many won't make it as long as they have a hole in their backside.*
> *Some are just scared of the responsibility of being good,*
> *Some are scared of their spouses and family,*
> *Who don't want a stronger version of them.*
> *Some are just so weak willed they don't have it in them.*
> *Most people blame the Instructor,*
> *Or family or work commitments,*
> *Or their relationship with other students,*
> *Or that 'the boss' (their spouse) won't let them.*
> *Or nagging injury or illness,*
> *Not realising that overcoming these problems is what makes a*
> *black belt.*
> *Some give up when they get a black belt.*
> *Not realising that is also a test.*
> *Black belt means beginner,*
> *It only means that you've found the ladder to climb.*
> *'Snatching defeat from the jaws of victory' describes them well.*
> *A black belt is an investment in a person.*
> *It is only a belt and a piece of paper*
> *Wearing it is another thing.*
> *Many martial artists don't realise they failed at that point.*

Taking responsibility for themselves,
Their own training,
Their own standards,
Their own progress,
Never blaming others for a setback,
Being strong enough to help others,
THAT's a black belt.

The traditional way of grading is with time periods, attendance record and formal examinations. I graded my students this way for many years. In the end I changed it to the following method:

- I don't charge for gradings because the connection of gradings and money does make it appear that it's just a money earner.
- We award all grades in class without any fuss including black belt because it's not about the belt, certificate or ego but to mark where the students are in the system.
- We use a method of continuous assessment, giving regular feedback to the students in class (sometimes with a feedback slip), usually in percentages as to where they are in regard to the next grade and what they need to work on to get there.
- We see the grades in this way for both student and teachers, so they know what class the student should be in and what they should be teaching them.

I like the grading system for these reasons and think that a continuous assessment is fairer than examinations because people progress at different rates and giving continuous feedback in class keeps everyone, both students and teachers, fully engaged with their progress. The student clearly understands what's required of them to move forward and they also know that as soon as they are ready they will get the grade. Moreover, and it's an honest assessment as there's no money involved.

Other teachers prefer the formal examinations because they feel that the pressure involved is an important part of the test. I think that the pressure doesn't relate to the different kinds of pressure a student will get in life and when confronting violence, and that it's not a good idea to give it all at once. Better to layer the different kinds of pressure gradually in class.

Grading doesn't mean much to anyone outside of a club/style/association/art, as the standards can vary considerable from one place to another. Karate is a broad church with clubs varying from Buddhist priest to street fighter. What it does do is to denote the relationship the student has with their instructor and where they are in their training system.

Training in karate is like the hands of a clock. The student doesn't see their improvement: often when they think that they're not progressing is when they are progressing the most, because they are struggling. Session after session, week after week, month after month, year after year, it's like putting pennies in the bank: you get rich with the skills, insight, knowledge and wisdom at a rate that's difficult to see at the time.

CHAPTER TWENTY

In Conclusion

Toru without a doubt played a huge part in turning me from a South London insensitive uneducated man into a self-educated, far more sensitive, cultured traditional karateka.

For that I write this book out of 'giri' (obligation) to him.

It's been twenty-five years since his passing and in the martial arts we tend to forget our real heroes too easily, as these days it seems that those that shout loudest get the most attention. It's up to us, however, to show who really affected the growth of our art and in an accurate light, as they are all only human.

While writing this book, I realised that there are many ideas I've had that I thought were unique insights of my own, only to realise that they were actually rooted in Toru's teachings – and for that I will be eternally grateful.

Domo arigatou gozaimasu Sensei.

Steve Rowe

SOFT FRONT
STRONG BACK

BUY IT NOW

Steve Rowe: Soft Front Strong Back
A Philosophy for Martial Arts, Business and Life
The Ran Network - The Budo Classics #4

It is Steve's ability to see the wood for the trees, to be frank about what you were not doing right, how to correct it in any number of different and engaging ways and not get bored. He was successful at improving everyone, young, old, bouncers, special forces and old school, traditional martial artists. This book encapsulates a lifetime of knowledge: read it, reread it, and read it again. You will be rewarded.
– Will Henshaw
Producer of BBC's Mind, Body & Kickass Moves

The books I've written in the past are either what a publisher asked and paid me to do, small instructional booklets for students, or poetry. Because of my philosophy expressed in magazine articles, blogs and posts, I've often been asked why I haven't written one on my philosophy, or in-depth on my martial arts. My answer has usually been that I like to express it in short bursts, so I do blogs and social media. However, I now feel it's time to record it with context from my life.
Why a soft front and a strong back? It encapsulates my entire philosophy. Fifty years of study has taught me that both, in balance, are necessary for a successful and happy life and business.
– Steve Rowe
Chief Instructor of Shi Kon Martial Arts International

Steve Rowe is a 73yr old 9th Dan black belt in martial arts with over 50 years study in the Arts, along with meditation, mindfulness, Taoism and Buddhism. He has lived a full life with his fair share of suffering and tragedy. For many years he has been teaching worldwide the philosophies presented in this book.

The Ran Network
https://therannetwork.com

Printed in Great Britain
by Amazon